T5-CVP-368

RAINBOW OF HOPE:

A Guide for the Special Needs Child

COVER ART

"Elena and Child" (Detail) by Edna Hibel, oil paint and gesso on board, courtesy Hibel Museum of Art, Palm Beach, Florida. Edna Hibel is widely known as America's most beloved and versatile artist, and a leader in advancing the causes of children. The Hibel Museum of Art is the world's only non-profit and publicly owned museum dedicated to the art of a living American woman.

RAINBOW OF HOPE:

A Guide for the Special Needs Child

Toby Levin

★ *Starlight*
PUBLISHING COMPANY INC.

RAINBOW OF HOPE: A Guide for the Special Needs Child
Copyright ©1992 by Toby Levin
All Rights Reserved

Printed in the United States of America. No part of this book
may be used or reproduced without written permission except
for the inclusion of brief passages in a review.

For further information: Starlight Publishing Company, Inc.
                           1893 N.E. 164 Street, Suite 100
                           North Miami Beach, FL 33162
                           Telephone (305) 944-8446

Library of Congress Catalog Number 91-67611

Publisher's Cataloging in Publication
(Prepared by Quality Books Inc.)

Levin, Toby.
    Rainbow of hope: a guide for the special needs child /
Toby Levin
    p. cm.
    Includes index.
    ISBN 0-9624680-1-0

    1. Handicapped children--Care--United States--Guide-
books. 2. Handicapped children--Education--United States--
Guide-books.   3. Handicapped children--Services for--
United States. 4. Abnormalities, Human--Psychological
aspects. I. Title

HV888.5.L4 1991   362.1
                                     QBI91-1825

10 9 8 7 6 5 4 3 2

Proceeds from the sale of this book will go to organizations
for CHILDREN WITH SPECIAL NEEDS.

This book is dedicated to all the children and their families who have to live with a disability. It is about Love for Today, HOPE FOR TOMORROW.

"There is only one child in the world and the child's name is All Children." – Carl Sandburg

CONTENTS

FOREWORD

In the small New England town where I grew up, a cemetery that was still in use included graves dating back to the late 1600s. Many an old plot consisted of paired headstones and footstones for husband and wife, intermingled with several little stones, not always inscribed, marking the graves of their offspring who died in infancy or childhood. Couples had large families then, and commonly lost one or more of their children, mostly to infectious diseases. Chronic infections like tuberculosis, and damage from acute infections were also a common cause of lasting disabilities.

Control of infectious diseases by hygienic measures, vaccines and antibiotics has been a triumph of social and scientific progress that we take for granted. In this country today, few of our children are lost to diphtheria or disabled by polio. As a result, birth defects have emerged by default as our leading cause of infant mortality and biggest child health problem.

Birth defects are not new, of course. Achondroplasia, a relatively common genetic form of dwarfism, appears in ancient Egyptian and Roman sculpture. Mesopotamian tablets 4,000 years old describe various congenital malformations, along with good and bad events that such births were believed to portend. In pre-Columbian times, Mayans, Incas and Aztecs recorded innumerable physical abnormalities, including birth defects, in their art.

Such records tell little or nothing about how people in ancient times coped with birth defects in themselves or their offspring, or behaved toward affected neighbors or strangers. They could not have done worse than some more recent societies in which anomalous births have too often been considered evidence of past personal sins. In the 17th Century, for example, a Danish woman whose baby was described as having a cat's head was burned alive, and in Connecticut, when a pig was born with one eye, a local man with one abnormal eye was blamed, and executed along with the pig.

Even today, parents of children with birth defects often suffer a form of superstitious blame by others, and by themselves. No doubt one reason is that scientific progress in understanding origins of some birth defects inclines people to overestimate both what is known, and the extent to which that knowledge enables prevention. Another reason is that when contemplating personal tragedies – be they heart attacks, rapes, or birth defects – we are tempted to believe that their causes are knowable and avoidable, because this belief offers hope that we can avoid such tragedies. But it also implies that heart attack or rape victims – or parents of children with birth defects – probably behaved in some unwise way to cause the problem. The emotional need to blame tragedy on some specific misbehavior can produce beliefs as farfetched as any ancient superstition. A recent caller to the March of Dimes, for example, was distressed by a strong hunch that her child's malformations were due to her having temporarily run out of bottled water early in pregnancy and drinking municipal tap water for a few days.

Such feelings are just one of many reasons for which new parents that are caught off-guard by birth defects need various kinds of informational and emotional support. They need to regain a measure of control of their own and their children's destinies. This book is a good way for them to start that process, and it points the way to many other resources that they can command.

Considerable effort may be needed to adapt one's place in a complex society to the needs of a child or grandchild with a birth defect. But many and varying resources are available, including some of the best people one could ever hope to meet under happier circumstances. We humans have unique ability to adapt the world to our normal needs and to various special ones. And we have an instinct to help each other, especially if someone reminds us firmly enough.

Like birth defects, that ability and instinct are parts of our nature that date back to ancient times. There is a 1987 report of an 11,000 year-old adult male skeleton found in an Italian cave, with clear evidence of a severe form of dwarfism that restricts movement, especially of the elbows. Whatever its original owner's talents may have been, he couldn't have participated much in the subsistence activities of a Stone Age hunter-gatherer group. Obviously he got what help he needed, and most likely gave something back too.

Richard Leavitt, Director of Science Information
March of Dimes Birth Defects Foundation

INTRODUCTION

New mothers can turn to baby books for information and guidance. But, when a baby is born with a disability, there is a need for answers to different questions.

This book was born out of that need – to help those families through a very difficult time by providing information about that disability, available services and support for them.

Whether your baby has a common or rare birth defect, you and your family are probably learning about it for the first time. This book is designed to answer some of the questions parents ask.

As a journalist, I am familiar with researching a subject. As I tried to learn more about my granddaughter's condition, I discovered facts that were overwhelming on a variety of issues. I realized that my information might help others in their time of need.

I started to write this book in 1989 and by the time I finished in 1991, there were extraordinary advances in genetics – advances that promise treatment and even cures for some of today's birth defects.

I have interviewed geneticists, medical experts, psychologists, and last but not least, the parents themselves. This book is above all about Love for Today and Hope for the Future.

CHAPTER 1

YOUR SPECIAL BABY

When Amy and Frank arrived at the hospital for the birth of their first baby, they wondered if it would be a boy or girl and were prepared with names.

What they weren't prepared for was the news their baby was born with a birth defect. They were suddenly forced to cope with a situation they were totally unprepared for.

The day their baby was diagnosed, they were overwhelmed with despair, heartbreak and confusion. That was their introduction to the world of birth defects.

The birth of a baby is a very special event and parents await its arrival with joyful anticipation. But, when your baby is born with a birth defect, that joy may turn to disbelief, anger, guilt and anguish. You feel as though it's only happening to you, but the reality is you are not alone.

One out of every 14 babies begins life with a birth defect and every year parents of some 250,000 American babies learn their child is one of the statistics.

The marvel is that the complex process of a new human

being works perfectly so much of the time. Birth defects can be caused by genetic or environmental factors as well as prematurity or problems connected with the actual birth. When chromosomal errors occur, especially during the formation of reproductive cells, the fertilized egg contains extra, missing or abnormally structured chromosomes. Once such an error occurs, it is repeated in the millions of cells that form the embryo, affecting a number of body functions.

Most parents who unexpectedly have a baby with a birth defect are said to follow a classic pattern of denial, grief, mourning and gradual acceptance of their child.

"There is pain in it," one mother said. "Parents must be permitted to mourn the child they expected and didn't get. Only then can they go on to accept their child."

According to a psychological casework study, "the mother's reaction to the loss of the healthy desired child is crushed by the birth of the defective one. The disappointment may be intensely felt but gradually diminishes to reduce the impact of the loss. This process, which requires time, can liberate the mother's feeling for a more realistic adaptation.

"There are two extreme reaction patterns. One is the guilt feeling where the mother dedicates herself to the child and the other is the impulse to deny relationship to the child because the underlying narcissistic injury is intolerable.

"Elements of denial and guilt are involved in parental reaction and only the reality of the child's condition helps them work through the mourning process and promotes adapting to the demands of reality. When a person is mourning, the ability to recognize and adapt to reality is often significantly impaired. Most parents gradually accept the situation and learn to deal with raising a special needs child." (Special needs are defined as any sensory, physical or mental disorder causing developmental delays or disabilities) Things settle down, routines are established and life goes on.

"I gave birth to the most beautiful baby in the world," one

2

mother said. "But, the next day, the bottom dropped out of my world when I was told she had a rare defect. Before that fateful day, I thought mental retardation was something that happened in other families."

"Our baby has taught us so much since she became part of our family," she adds. "We learned first of all that life goes on. As the days passed and we became acquainted with our baby, we found she needed the same things any baby needs – love, cuddling, feeding and diapers changed. We adjusted and our routine began to feel normal, even though it included infant stimulation and other therapies. By the time she was three years old, she could walk, talk with a limited vocabulary and was the light of our lives."

WHY ME?

When parents learn their baby has a birth defect, they often ask the predictable question, "Why me?"

Opera singer Beverly Sills asked the same question when her daughter, Muffy, was born deaf. The irony of having a child who could never hear her music was so great she was almost paralyzed by her pain. When her mother threatened to take the child away if she didn't snap out of it, the opera star enrolled her daughter in a pre-school program for the deaf. Two years later, Beverly Sills got another shock when she gave birth to a son, diagnosed as deaf and retarded as well as autistic. She now tours the country sharing her experiences with other parents and professionals and says there are many more services available to all families today so they can learn to cope.

Most parents eventually go from asking "why" to "what do I do now?"

"I know when you have a child with a birth defect, you suddenly feel like it's the end of the world," another mother said. "The hopes and dreams you once had for your child are shattered. But, believe me, time heals the hurt and as they grow and develop into their own little personalities, you learn to love them more than ever."

Psychiatrists have studied how couples react to the birth of a premature or ill baby to determine what helps some adapt more successfully than others. They found those who expressed their feelings and accepted help from family and friends in handling the problems were most successful. It also helped for parents to get together with other parents of a handicapped child who "have been there."

Sometimes it is helpful to seek out a minister, priest or rabbi, go for professional counseling or find comfort in certain books. One such book was on the New York Times Bestseller List for eight months.

"When Bad Things Happen to Good People" was written by Rabbi Harold S. Kushner when personal tragedy struck and his son was diagnosed with a progressively fatal disease, progeria or "rapid aging." Like most people, he says, he was aware of human tragedies. But when he heard the news, he thought, "This can't be happening. It's not how the world is supposed to work."

He asked the same universal question Why? for the ten years he lived with the knowledge his son was doomed by a disease. He decided to write the book to help others who find themselves in a similar predicament and in memory of his son "whose life made it possible and because his death made it necessary."

WHEN YOU FIND OUT

There is no typical way to find out your baby has a birth defect. In some cases it's obvious immediately as in Down syndrome or spina bifida, while in others the diagnosis may not be made for weeks, months or even years.

Babies with a suspected or confirmed diagnosis may be sent home with the mother if there are no physical problems as well. Babies who are seriously ill may require hospitalization and testing before they are ready to go home. Others who seem perfectly normal at birth don't develop problems until later.

Although it may be difficult to tell how a child is developing, there are certain basic timetables. Smiling is a benchmark since delayed babies may not smile until much later than a normal baby who responds to a smile by smiling back as young as a month old. If a baby shows lack of growth and development by six months, begin by consulting your baby's doctor. An examination or tests for early diagnosis is important. Earlier detection means earlier therapies to maximize development.

"My baby was seven months old before the diagnosis was made," said one mother. "As soon as her condition was confirmed, we began therapy. When she was two, we started her in a parent infant program, then in a state-funded private school followed by a special education program in the public school system."

The first year is the greatest learning period for all babies. Development combines physical, mental and emotional patterns that babies follow with their individual timetables.

Infants who have stimulation will have better developed abilities than those who don't. This is the reason institutionalized children developed so poorly in the past. Interaction that takes place between a baby and its caregivers is a vital link to development. When babies lacked holding and fondling at institutions, they became retarded in all areas. Unfortunately, medical professionals at many hospitals have access only to information describing children with a particular defect who were institutionalized. In the last decade or more, there have been improvements in treatment and new reports offer much

5

more hope.

Today, even the most serious birth defects have a potential beyond what was previously thought possible. Parental love, care and educational support all have a direct relationship to the degree that potential is reached.

NO ONE SENT US FLOWERS

Just as there is no typical way to find out about your baby's disorder, there is no typical way to tell others about it. Friends often don't know how to react when they find out. In most cases, no one sends you flowers.

One confused friend turned to Dear Abby and asked what to do. She didn't know whether to send a card or baby gift to someone who had such a tragedy and wondered if the situation called for a message of sympathy or no acknowledgement at all. The reply was "that a child, normal or otherwise, is a child to its mother." The advice was not to differentiate but to send a little gift with love and best wishes.

Another letter came from a mother who had a baby born with spina bifida and responded to the "confused friend." She told Abby that they were delighted with their baby and were still waiting to hear from friends she suspects also don't know what to say. She reported receiving sympathy cards and messages she considered inappropriate and advises people to do everything they would have done had the baby arrived without a problem.

One letter was signed by a "proud grandmother" whose daughter had a baby with Down syndrome and realized many people would be perplexed. She enclosed a note with each birth announcement explaining that their son was born with Down syndrome and there was no easy way to say it. She hoped they would accept him without pity or reservations and to ask her any questions they might have.

The birth of a baby is all in the family and affects siblings, grandparents and other relatives as well as the parents. Special children have special families who have to cope with the new situation that has entered their lives. When one premature baby was born in 1960 with a brain injury that caused cerebral palsy, the entire extended family was affected.

"Debbie has not brought me the heartache that was described by her doctor initially," her grandfather said. "She has done just the opposite and given me the most intense kind of joy and pleasure that any man could experience."

Small wonder that he had the vision to help establish The Mailman Center for Child Development at the University of Miami Medical School in Miami, Florida, that bears his name. Established in 1970, the evaluation center services developmentally disabled children ranging in age from birth to 20. The main tower houses clinical and research facilities and is connected to the Debbie Institute, named after A.L. Mailman's granddaughter, to provide special programs for the children.

"We would never wish anyone a brain-injured child, but our whole family has been enriched through the experience of living with Debbie," said her mother, Dr. Marilyn Segal, professor of developmental psychology and Dean of the Family Center at Nova University in Fort Lauderdale, Florida. She is also the author of "Run Away Little Girl", a first-hand account of a family's love and devotion in raising a special child.

No one ever said that raising a handicapped child is easy. But, once the family adjusts to living with the child, a routine is established that may include various therapy sessions. It takes patience and skill combined with love and hope. Special needs children need special parents and special services. Many parents say that even with all the difficulties, they love their child deeply. In the words of one young mother, "I wouldn't trade my son for all the diamonds in

Bangkok."

The following is an anonymous letter printed in a newsletter of a national support group.

"I love you, dear child in my arms. I did not wish for you to have something like Williams syndrome. I took good care of me while I was carrying you so that together we would face things like diaper rash, skinned knees, mean teachers, boys who didn't call and demanding mother-in-laws. I truly did not hope for you that you would have failure to thrive, selective eating problems, a heart defect, learning problems, sensitivity to sound and surgery and disappointments. I wanted to help you conquer the world that I knew. But, together we will conquer the world that you know. I have met others with your problem and I have seen them do well, little one. They are loving and kind, friendly and outgoing, sensitive and caring. They do not give up easily, nor do I. Together you and I will overcome this challenge. You will be all my new dreams come true. And yours."

WHERE TO GO FOR HELP

After the diagnosis is confirmed about your baby's specific birth defect, get all the information you can from the hospital staff and contact their social services office.

Then check with organizations dealing with the same or a similar condition. A first step might be to check your local phone book (customer guide on the first pages) for human services information and referral.

Another good start is to contact your local or national March of Dimes chapter. From 1938 to 1958, the March of Dimes set out to conquer infantile paralysis (polio). After that disease was conquered, the focus changed to fighting birth defects and in 1979, the name was officially changed to The March of Dimes Birth Defects Foundation. This unique partnership of volunteers and professionals in the treatment and prevention of birth defects, prematurity and infant mortality, provides families with information through programs supported by its local chapters. See the Resource Section at the back of the book for further information.

CHAPTER 2

ABOUT BIRTH DEFECTS

Four million babies are born in the United States each year. Unfortunately, many will come into the world with some problem.

A birth defect is a seen or unseen disorder that exists at birth caused by prematurity, genetic or environmental factors and strikes those of all races and ethnic backgrounds from all walks of life.

"One out of every 30 babies born in the United States has an immediately identifiable defect, likely to be genetic," according to Dr. Karl Muench, chief of genetic medicine at the University of Miami Medical School. There are about 4000 genetically linked diseases.

An abnormality of structure, function or body metabolism may result in physical or mental handicaps, shorten life or prove fatal. A large number of chromosomal abnormalities vary greatly in severity and body functions they affect. Some are relatively common while others are rare and can be inherited or occur sporadically. Not all inherited disorders are apparent at birth and the age when symptoms appear

11

differs greatly.

Hereditary information is passed from parent to child by genes located in the chromosomes found in every body cell. Every normal person has 23 pairs or a total of 46 chromosomes per cell. The reproductive cells (egg and sperm) contain 23 unpaired chromosomes each, but at fertilization a single cell with the full chromosome count is formed.

Genes carry the blueprint for everything from eye color to height but tragically also for inherited disease. Everyone has a few potentially harmful recessive genes in their genetic makeup. In some cases one parent has a single faulty gene which dominates its normal counterpart and each child has a 50 percent chance of inheriting the faulty dominant gene and the defect.

In other genetic disorders, both apparently normal parents carry the same abnormal recessive gene and each child has a 25 percent risk of receiving that gene from both parents and the consequent defect, a 50 percent chance of being an unaffected carrier and a 25 percent chance of receiving the normal gene from both parents. Autosomal recessive inherited diseases tend to be more severe, may cause death early in life and often occur more frequently in offspring of parents who are related to each other or both members of the same ethnic group.

Many genetic diseases, such as Tay-Sachs, occur as a result of historical and geographical circumstances. Descendants of central and Eastern European Jews are primarily affected and carriers of this disease. One in 25 American Jews carries the Tay-Sachs gene,and if both parents are carriers, there is a one in four chance their baby will have two copies of the gene and therefore the disease.

Mutations and chromosomal abnormalities are changes in the genetic material of sperm and egg cells or embryonic body cells that may occur as spontaneous mistakes. In chromosomal disorders, there may be too many or too few chromosomes per cell, part of one may be missing (deleted) or broken off and reattached to another chromosome (translocated). When a chromosomal error occurs in a sperm or egg, it affects that pregnancy and there is very little risk that a similar accident will affect later conceptions.

The possibility of certain of these errors is significantly higher in a woman's later reproductive years. As she gets older, chances increase that a mishap will occur during maturation of an egg prior to its fertilization and she is at increased risk of having a child with a birth defect due to an extra chromosome.

Down syndrome occurs in one out of 1,250 babies born to women in their 20's. By age 35, chances increase to one in 365; at age 40, to one in 110; and at 45, to one in 30.

A syndrome by definition is a collection of abnormalities that go together to form a recognizable pattern. The diagnosis is made by demonstrating that the affected person has the hallmark characteristics of the syndrome.

In general, birth defects fall into various categories. Chromosomal abnormalities result in Down syndrome and hundreds of other conditions usually involving some combination of mental retardation and physical malformations. At least one in 300 children is born with some chromosome problem and chromosomal errors cause about 50 percent of miscarriages.

Malformations present at birth include structural defects like spina bifida (open spine) and cleft palate. Inborn errors of metabolism (body chemistry) cause such disorders as Tay-Sachs and cystic fibrosis, resulting from the inability of body cells to produce the right amounts or forms of certain enzymes or other proteins.

Perinatal damage may be caused by infections, drugs or other agents and most commonly, premature birth. Blood disorders include sickle cell anemia, thalassemia and hemophilia, due to a missing, reduced or abnormal blood component.

Some 250 disorders are sex-linked and transmitted by a gene or genes on the X chromosome (females have two X chromosomes, males have one X and one Y). An apparently normal mother may have an abnormal gene on one of her X chromosomes with a 50 percent chance of its being inherited by any son. For example, hemophilia is passed from carrier mother to a male child since he only has one X chromosome. A daughter who inherits the abnormal X chromosome is a carrier, very seldom affected because the healthy X chromosome from her father overrides the deleterious effect. There may be a missing (in females) or extra (in males) X chromosome, resulting in certain syndromes affecting growth and sexual development.

Of every 100 babies, two are born with a serious defect for which no specific cause can be identified. Some are caused by environmental factors such as drugs or chemicals. More than 3000 different disorders cause mental and/or physical defects. There is usually no cure, only management or treatment, but significant medical improvements offer a brighter future for many children born with a birth defect today. In the last decade of the 20th Century, there will be giant inroads leading to some potential cures.

COMMON BIRTH DEFECTS

DOWN SYNDROME

It is the most common chromosomal disorder, occurring in one out of every 800 births and is the major known genetic cause of mental retardation in the United States. Although not commonly known, 80 percent of Down syndrome babies are born to women under 35. Between 4000 and 5000 babies are born with Down syndrome each year in the United States.

14

In 1959, Dr. Jerome Lejeune discovered that an extra copy of chromosome 21 causes Down syndrome, originally called mongolism because most infants have a somewhat Oriental appearance. In addition to oval shaped eyes, they tend to have a short neck, oversized tongue, flat nose and malformations of the heart and other organs.

The degree of mental retardation varies from mild to severe. They do most things other children do, but they do it much later. Early intervention helps them live up to their potential.

It is caused by an extra chromosome contributed either by the egg or sperm cell. Although there is no cure at the present time, thanks to new technology, researchers are able to focus on chromosome 21 with its approximately 1000 genes. It is a prototype of a federal gene mapping project intent on finding the defect and ways to correct it.

National Down Syndrome Society was established in 1979 to promote better understanding, support research and provide services. Another important function is to communicate state-of-the-art information and ongoing research to the health care community as well as to families. A list of early intervention programs and parent groups in each state is available and an 800 hotline provides information and referral to resources throughout the country. Call 1(800)221-4602 for a free information packet. National Down Syndrome Congress has more than 500 chapters in the United States and in many foreign countries, serving as a clearinghouse and making referrals to local chapters or resources.

CYSTIC FIBROSIS

It is the number one genetic killer of American children affecting one in every 2,500 births. It affects the lungs, pancreas and sweat glands. Keeping the lungs clear and preventing infections is a daily battle.

15

It is caused by a recessive gene from both parents. At least one out of every 25 Caucasian Americans carries one copy of the gene, although most people don't know it.

One of the most exciting discoveries in the history of genetic research was discovery of the cystic fibrosis gene and identifying the abnormal protein it creates.

While no cure exists at the moment, researchers in 1989 were able to pinpoint the usual defect in the gene that causes the disease by knowing where it maps on chromosome seven. This was an enormous breakthrough and opened the way for screening tests to determine which couples are at risk. In the past, there was no way to know until a couple had a cystic fibrosis child. Improvements in treating the disease, with the ultimate goal of control and cure, are closer than ever.

Since Cystic Fibrosis Foundation was established in 1955, tremendous advances in treatment have improved the outlook for those with the dreadful disease. Over 120 care centers across the country provide special care. The Cystic Fibrosis Foundation has aggressively supported state-of-the-art research in its American and Canadian centers by creating the strategy for unraveling the complex nature of this disease.

CEREBRAL PALSY

It is the number one lifetime disabling condition resulting from damage to the brain, usually occurring before, during or shortly after birth and affects the central nervous system. A developmental disability may result from mental or physical impairment, or both.

About 8,000 babies are born each year with disorders resulting in cerebral (brain) palsy (disorder of movement). It is often caused by lack of oxygen to the brain and is not hereditary. About one third of cerebral palsy babies are born prematurely and one half have some degree of mental retardation.

16

The infant with cerebral palsy may feed poorly and have very slow development of muscular control and coordination. Management treatment helps the child live up to its potential.

United Cerebral Palsy is a nationwide network of approximately 200 state and local affiliates serving children and their families. Although it focuses on this particular condition, services are open to anyone with a developmental disability.

PREMATURE BABIES

About 400,000 babies are born prematurely every year. Preterm birth is a major factor in low birth weight, which refers to babies born weighing less than 5 pounds, 8 ounces. Some low birth weight babies who survive may have mental or physical disabilities. Breathing problems caused by premature birth can deprive the brain of oxygen.

Early, regular prenatal care is the most important factor in preventing low birth weight. About 80 percent of high risk women can be identified on the first prenatal visit and risk-lowering interventions can begin. Not enough can be said about the importance of prenatal care.

Fetal monitoring during labor may help avoid problems leading to brain damage. Special facilities for high risk newborns can help maintain oxygen flow and deal with other critical care problems.

MENTAL RETARDATION

It is the result of genetic irregularities, problems during pregnancy or birth and environmental factors. Over 100,000 babies born each year in the United States are found to be mentally retarded. This makes one out of every 10 Americans involved with the disability by having a mentally retarded relative.

People with mental retardation (under 70 IQ) fall into mild

17

(above 55 IQ) moderate (35-54 IQ), severe (20-34 IQ) and profound (below 20 IQ) categories. They form the largest group of people with a disability.

It is caused by many conditions which impair development of the brain. Hereditary components are known to account for only a fraction of cases. There are over 250 known causes, but they account for only about 25 percent. In the other 75 percent, the specific cause is still unknown or unexplained.

Association of Retarded Citizens is the largest volunteer organization solely devoted to improving the welfare of children and adults with mental retardation. Formed in 1950 by a small group of parents, the grass root organization today has over 1300 state and local chapters in the United States, providing services for families and helping local communities meet the needs of children from birth to three years.

SPINA BIFIDA

It is a defect of the spinal column (open spine) and one of the most common neural tube defects, affecting at least one in 2000 babies in the United States each year. Neural tube defects are malformations apparent at birth. Children may have mental retardation and other problems depending upon the location of the defect.

The exact cause is not known and may result from a combination of causes. Parents are not carriers of a gene that specifically causes spina bifida, though they may carry genes which make offspring susceptible to various environmental factors. The chance of having a second child with this condition is about one in 40.

Spina Bifida Association of America has operated an information clearinghouse since 1975 and has a referral toll free number 1(800) 621-3141.

18

HYDROCEPHALUS (WATER ON THE BRAIN)

It is a result of fluid that collects resulting in an enlarged head. It is caused by a defect in drainage of fluid from the brain or in the membrane supposed to absorb the fluid around the brain, and often occurs with spina bifida or other causes.

ANENCEPHALY

It is a neural tube defect affecting brain development by failure of the neural tube to fuse in its uppermost portion early in pregnancy. Most affected fetuses are miscarried; about half of 1000 to 2000 anencephalic babies born in the United States each year are stillborn and the rest die within days or weeks.

THALASSEMIA

It is one of the most common blood disorders passed on by autosomal recessive inheritance when both parents are carriers. Most are of Mediterranean, black or Asian descent. Children usually appear healthy at birth but, as early as one year of age, they become pale and prone to many infections. Without treatment, heart failure and infections may lead quickly to death.

Blood tests and family genetic studies can show if an individual has thalassemia or is a carrier, and it can be detected by amniocentesis. Recent March of Dimes supported research corrected the genetic defect in a test tube experiment, and researchers are exploring various approaches to effective gene treatment. The most severe type of this defect in production of red blood cells is Cooley's anemia.

SICKLE CELL ANEMIA

It is an inherited blood disorder with one defective gene from each parent who is a carrier. Most cases occur among blacks and Hispanics of Caribbean ancestry. About one in every 500 American blacks and one in every 1000 to 1500 Hispanics inherit the disease.

It can cause damage to vital organs and sometimes death. In affected people, hemoglobin tends to clump together and distort red blood cells into sickle shapes. A test is available to identify those who have the trait or the disease.

AUTISM

It is a developmental disability that occurs in 5-15 births per 10,000. Children are withdrawn and tend to avoid interacting with others.

It is mostly caused by unknown factors affecting brain development and is more common in boys. The brain of an autistic person shows reduced size of the cerebellum and this finding may point the way to understanding the development of parts of the brain that control language and sensory information. It may sometimes be the result of a recessive gene from both parents. Nearly one half of all autistic children have some other condition affecting the central nervous system.

CONGENITAL HEART DEFECTS

It is present at birth in at least one out of every 175 babies and may be part of a pattern of defects such as in Down syndrome children, where some 50 percent are affected.

It is caused by certain infections or chemicals as well as some abnormalities and many children are helped by surgery or medication.

CONGENITAL VISION AND HEARING IMPAIRMENT

It is caused by genetic disorders, metabolic diseases or congenital abnormalities. An isolated gene is involved in retinitis pigmentosa, a leading cause of blindness. Retinal dystrophy is a genetic disease that causes progressive deterioration of the eye, resulting in blindness.

There are more than 200 known genetic forms of hearing impairment with approximately 3,000 impaired babies born each year. Hearing problems usually occur with other handicapping conditions.

NEUROFIBROMATOSIS

It is an inherited skin and nervous system disorder that may disfigure the body and face at some point in life in one out of every 4,000 people in the United States. Common early signs are coffee-colored spots on the skin and later small tumors begin to develop that can cause disfigurement, paralysis, blindness, deafness and cancer.

It is caused by an abnormal dominant gene inherited from one parent who has the disease or the result of a spontaneous genetic mutation which accounts for half the cases.

SEX-LINKED DISORDERS

Some disorders are "sex-linked" resulting from a defect on the X chromosome (females have two X, males have one X and one Y.) A woman needs two copies of the defective gene to get the disease because she has one healthy gene to compensate for the other. If a man inherits a gene for the disease on his X chromosome, he will get the disease because he has nothing to compensate for it.

DUCHENNE MUSCULAR DYSTROPHY

It is an X-linked degenerative disease that strikes one in 3,500 male children, usually resulting in death during the second decade of life. It is the most common and serious of genetically caused muscular dystrophy with a high frequency of mild mental retardation.

This gene is susceptible to spontaneous mutation and it is estimated that one third of all sufferers are born to noncarrier mothers of the faulty gene. It's cause was unknown until 1986 when scientists found and decoded the gene which is the blueprint for a structural protein found in muscles. With the gene decoded, they were able to identify the protein, dystrophin, that the healthy gene produces. The defective Duchenne gene produces either an abnormal form or none at all. This landmark discovery opened the door to treatment and possible cure.

FRAGILE X SYNDROME

It is the most common inherited form of mental retardation, occurring in one out of 1,000 males. Unlike other X-linked disorders, it also affects females (about one in 2,000). The gene that cause FXS is located on the X chromosome and is passed from mother to son. It derives its name from the presence of an unusual chromosomal finding called the fragile site. In addition to mental impairment, there are behaviors and physical characteristics.

HEMOPHILIA

It is caused by a gene passed by the mother to a male child resulting in failure of the blood to clot quickly enough due to lack of a clotting protein. It occurs in one out of 10,000 males and in severe cases it causes prolonged and uncontrollable bleeding from even the slightest cut. The gene was cloned in 1984, paving the way for treatment.

KLINEFELTER SYNDROME

It is caused by an extra X chromosome that occurs in one out of 1,000 male births worldwide. It is often not diagnosed until a boy is near adolescent age.

RETT SYNDROME

It is found in females and occurs in one out of every 15,000 births. Although it is a neurological disorder, the cause of the syndrome is unknown.

TURNER SYNDROME

It is found in females who have one X chromosome instead of the normal two and occurs in one out of every 2,500 births. It is usually associated with growth problems, failure of puberty and infertility.

FETAL ALCOHOL SYNDROME

One baby in 750 is born with a serious combination of birth defects to women who drink while pregnant. FAS is a leading cause of mental retardation. Impaired ability and physical problems are the legacy these children receive. It is preventable and attention is called to the dangers of drinking while pregnant.

A 1988 act of Congress requires liquor bottle labels to include a warning to pregnant women. It reads "GOVERNMENT WARNING: According to the Surgeon General, women should not drink alcoholic beverages during pregnancy because of the risk of birth defects".

COCAINE BABIES

According to reports at a 1990 Symposium on birth defects, one out of ten babies born to women who abuse drugs will have a birth defect.

Recent studies indicate that babies born to mothers who smoke crack cocaine during pregnancy have learning deficits similar to those caused by alcohol. In 1990, 300,000 babies were born to drug-abusing mothers. In many cases, the brain is affected as it matures in the womb. It is estimated there may be as many as 4 million such children with serious developmental problems by the year 2000.

UNCOMMON BIRTH DEFECTS

ACHONDROPLASIA

It is one of the oldest recorded birth defects and occurs in one out of some 20,000 births. The genetic disorder of bone growth affects the growth of long bones and causes extreme shortness of arms and legs.

It is caused by an abnormal dominant gene passed from parent to child but in 80 percent of cases, it is caused by a new mutation and parents are average-sized.

More than 80 different birth defects cause bones to grow disproportionately. Approximately 15,000 children have growth failure due to growth hormone deficiency resulting from the absence or inadequacy of the growth hormone necessary for normal growth. It may result from abnormal formation of the pituitary or hypothalamus before birth or from damage during or after birth. Many genetic syndromes are associated with growth problems. A few can be treated with injections of growth hormone. The first biosynthetic growth hormone was approved for use by the FDA in 1985.

MARFAN SYNDROME

It is a disorder of connective tissue that holds tissue to the body and affects one out of 10,000 births in the United States. Symptoms may be present at birth or show up later. Features of the disorder are abnormally long fingers and limbs with heart and blood vessels also affected.

It is caused by a single abnormal gene or in about 15 percent of cases, by a new mutation.

HUNTINGTON'S DISEASE

It is an inherited progressively degenerative brain disorder caused by a single dominant gene in one out of 20,000 Americans. Symptoms don't appear until later in life with mental and physical deterioration that often leads to death, as in the case of folk singer Woody Guthrie.

At the present time there is no effective treatment or cure. Since researchers discovered a genetic marker on the fourth chromosome, a test was developed in 1986 to identify many who will develop the disease.

PHENYLKETONURIA

It is an inherited metabolic disorder affecting one in 14,000 babies in their ability to process food. If not treated, it causes mental retardation. But, once diagnosed, treatment consists of a special diet.

The first newborn screening test made available was for PKU in the 1960's. Today, all babies are screened at the hospital.

PRADER-WILLI SYNDROME

It is a chromosomal or genetic disorder of one in 10,000

births, although it is sometimes not recognized until late childhood. Signs often present at birth include floppy muscle tone and poor sucking response. First described in 1956, it usually occurs sporadically with a small chromosome 15 deletion. The complex syndrome has multiple medical, behavioral and education features.

CRI DU CHAT SYNDROME (CRY OF THE CAT)

It is a result of genetic material loss (deletion) from a region of chromosome 5 and may be identified by the distinct cry at birth. The cause is unknown and occurs in approximately one in 50,000 newborns each year.

WILLIAMS SYNDROME

It is recognized by the hallmark characteristics of the syndrome which are elfin, pixie-like features, cardiac problems and mental retardation. Occurring in one out of 20,000 births, it cannot be determined before birth and usually isn't diagnosed until the child appears delayed and has other symptoms as well.

The cause is still unknown and has appeared as a sporadic event in otherwise normal families.

RARE DEFECTS

By definition a condition is rare if it strikes fewer than 200,000 people. There are approximately 5,000 rare diseases in the United States, the majority of which are genetic. Those with these "orphan" diseases often have no place to go for help because there is no specific organization for them and little information about the latest treatment and drugs.

TAY-SACHS

Tay-Sachs and the allied diseases are rare genetic diseases that primarily affect young children and are known collectively as lysosomal storage diseases.

Tay-Sachs is the best known example of this group, resulting from a deficiency of an enzyme necessary for the body cells to dispose of certain metabolic waste products. Although babies appear normal at birth, it causes progressive destruction of the central nervous system with symptoms first appearing at about six months and then worsens until death by three to five years.

Descendants of Central and Eastern European Jews are primarily affected and nearly one out of 25 American Jews is a carrier. When two carriers become parents, there is a one-in-four chance their child will inherit the disease. Wide-scale carrier screening and prenatal diagnosis is available.

Gaucher's disease is the most common of the lipid storage disorders and becomes apparent in childhood or early adulthood. In 1991, a drug developed by Genzyme and approved by the FDA, replaces a missing enzyme.

TOURETTE'S SYNDROME

It is a neurological disorder believed to affect the chemical balance of neurotransmitters in the brain and is characterized by tics. For over 100,000 Americans who have the disease, it generally begins in childhood. Genetic studies indicate the syndrome is inherited as a dominant gene and medication to alter the brain's chemistry appears to help.

BATTEN'S DISEASE

It is a recessive inherited disorder of the nervous system and manifests itself in previously normal children at about five to ten years of age. The exact enzyme defect and its cause are unknown but the progressive disorder always ends in death. *It is* probably the most common of the neurogenetic storage diseases in a group of neurologic disorders.

WILSON'S DISEASE

It is a rare genetic disorder characterized by excess storage of copper in the body tissues and is fatal if not treated in time. It is a recessively inherited disease that is difficult to diagnose. When the marker for Wilson's disease is found, it will be possible to identify carriers and to diagnose those with the disease earlier.

XERODERMA PIGMENTOSUM

It is a rare, usually fatal, genetic disease that literally robs its victims of the sunlight. Even if briefly exposed to the sun, they are vulnerable to eye and skin cancers. Unlike normal people, they lack the ability to repair damage sunlight does to DNA in cells.

The recessive inherited disorder affects one in 200,000 people in the United States. There is no test presently to show whether a person carries the trait, but researchers are studying XP in hopes of finding the defective enzyme.

Although the disorders named above have their own organizations, there are many others that don't. One organization that can help is the National Information Center for Orphan Drugs and Rare Diseases (NICODRD) that answers questions about rare disorders and helps locate support groups.

The National Organization for Rare Disorders is dedicated to the identification and improved treatment of rare diseases. NORD believes the first step in conquering them must begin by familiarizing the medical professions with the diagnosis and current treatment of these little known disorders since much of the medical literature is inaccurate or outdated.

CHAPTER 3

YOU ARE NOT ALONE

Many parents who find their baby has a birth defect feel so alone. It is helpful to get together with other parents who "have been there" since they can be especially understanding and an invaluable source of practical information.

Professionals involved in dealing with birth defects say parents told them how much they would have welcomed an opportunity, especially in the beginning, to meet other parents who have a child with a similar disability.

The Association for Children with Down Syndrome offers this message to new parents:

"We know and we understand. We have been where you are. We can show you that this is not the end of your world, only a different beginning."

"Please know that you are not alone. Others have learned to overcome the initial shock, adjust their preconceived notions and discover a new set of values. Right now you may be full of fears, doubts and bitterness, but your feelings will change after you have given your newborn a chance. Investigate every aspect of the situation, confer with others, particularly parents of children

31

like yours."

SUPPORT GROUPS

By definition a self-help group is composed of people who share a common concern and help each other cope in their everyday lives by providing emotional support, sharing experiences, knowledge, advice and hope.

These "support groups" respond to the needs of families in areas of therapies, education, research and medical treatment. This information is invaluable for new families who have just learned about their child's condition and continues as their needs change.

One of the most important functions is to reach into the medical, scientific and professional communities for referral of newly diagnosed individuals to encourage research aimed at finding causes and possible cures.

Families learn from one another and provide professionals access to their group. It is a symbiotic relationship since researchers get invaluable first-hand observation.

"A support group is the only method of healing the parent," says Kay Biescar, mother of a Williams Syndrome child and administrative assistant of the Williams Syndrome Association.

What began as a small parent group in southern California in 1982 has grown to over 1600 families in the United States and there are groups around the world.

Its goal is to provide support for families and give professionals access to the group for study as well as to locate other families unaware of the association. A new membership directory has been printed to help families find others living nearby.

A handbook incorporating ideas for both parents and teachers, based on those originally developed in England, is a top priority and will be useful for those diagnosed in the future. As a direct result of efforts by several support groups, there have been major changes in how some birth defects are being diagnosed.

The WSA held its fourth national family convention in Boston, Massachusetts, in August, 1990, preceded by a professional symposium to encourage research and a multidisciplinary approach to the syndrome.

Defects like Williams syndrome are uncommon and it may be difficult to find an existing support group. One desperate mother wrote to Ann Landers in an effort to find other parents to share information and start up a group.

Her son had Klinefelter's syndrome. She had talked to many people in the medical profession, but did not learn much from them since limited information is available for some disorders.

"When my child was diagnosed in 1975, I was told he had Prader-Willi syndrome," another mother said. "I was also told there was no literature and no hope. The only thing that helped me was when a psychologist showed me something about a Prader-Willi Syndrome group. That was the first support I had."

The Prader-Willi Syndrome Association began with 140 members in 1975 and has grown to over 5000 with 32 chapters in the United States and groups in Canada and other countries as well. A PWSA conference held in Salt Lake City, Utah, in 1990, brought together parents and professionals to share information.

"The professionals usually just see these children briefly," said Rosella Van Swearingen. "This is an opportunity for them to spend more time and observe more of them. We parents live with the children all the time."

Other parent-to-parent programs are sponsored by established organizations such as United Cerebral Palsy and Association for Retarded Citizens. The March of Dimes encourages support groups and over 100 have been formed with their assistance.

National organizations for specific disorders providing services for families and parent support groups include National Down Syndrome Society, Spina Bifida Association and National Tay-Sachs and Allied Diseases Association. The Alliance of Genetic Support Groups is a national coalition of support groups and involved professionals whose goal is to establish an international data base.

A small group of parents who all had a child afflicted with Tay-Sachs, a rare fatal genetic disease, founded that organization in 1958. Today, it reaches thousands with support to families, access to a directory of other parents, promotes carrier screening and helps locate health and human services. The parent peer support group extends worldwide and is coordinated by parent volunteers.

Spina Bifida Association represents over 100 local chapters with support systems for parents. National Down Syndrome Society provides a list of parent groups in each state and offers materials written primarily to answer new parents' most immediate questions.

The National Organization for Rare Diseases (NORD) refers those with rare disorders to support groups where they exist. If there is none for a specific disease, they may enroll in NORD's Networking program. By linking people with the same disorder, NORD encourages formation of new support groups for even the rarest disorders.

The Networking program evolved from an informal pen pal situation to an international self-help effort. Families have developed their own communication methods to keep in touch and can also benefit from NORD's newsletter which reports about progress in research and recent activities by government and health related industries.

Parents of Down syndrome children (PODS) is a group in Miami, Florida, that first met at a series of classes on self-help skills. They recognized they could be of great help to each other and continue meeting once a month in different areas of the county.

"Remembering our frightened feelings of panic, anger and grief, we all felt that if only we could have found another parent to talk to and ask questions, maybe our adjustment would have been easier," said Sylvia Sanchez, PODS parent-to-parent coordinator.

"Sometimes even today, well-meaning friends, relatives or professionals may suggest that institutional care is the wisest choice," she says. "Our children are being raised at home and we believe we have made the wisest choice for ourselves and our children. Before considering alternatives, grant yourselves the opportunity to recover from the shock."

Fallacies about Down syndrome as well as other birth defects arose in the past because of early institutionalization. Many children were confined to cribs and never provided stimulation or the opportunity to learn.

Modern thinking is to start infant stimulation and therapy as early as possible. Some private schools for exceptional children accept developmentally disabled infants as young as six weeks and public school classes are also available.

Most communities have parent support groups and programs have been implemented by many states since 1980 with all states planning to provide family support services. The purpose of most state programs is to keep individuals at risk in a family setting at home instead of placement in an institution.

LOOKING IN

For an in-depth look at a support group, I will focus on Cri-du-Chat syndrome children and their parents who meet at annual national meetings.

Because it is rare and not much is known, families rely on

each other and guest speakers for information. That is the main purpose, but it is much more than that. It is a chance to see other children with the same syndrome, meet their parents and siblings and share feelings and ideas that only another parent can understand. The get-togethers provide a rare opportunity to see children of all ages with the syndrome.

The first get-together was held at a park in West Bend, Wisconsin, in 1983, with six families. The following year, seven families met for an entire weekend and had time for discussions and planning. By the third meeting in 1985, there were 15 families, including Kent and Edie Nicholls.

Kent, who was president and helped found the support group, works for Apple Computer and was determined to broaden its scope through use of his computer knowledge. To prepare for the next meeting, he sent letters to doctors, hospitals and genetic departments all over the world, in addition to a computerized list for the families.

By the fourth meeting in 1986, there were 30 families gathered to hear Dr. Louise Wilkins, author of a landmark four-year study of Cri-du-Chat children, and Dr. Mary Carlin who wrote about the medical and physical aspects in The Improved Prognosis in Cri-du-Chat (5p-Syndrome.)

"Most individuals born prior to 1970 were institutionalized and many died at early ages of respiratory, cardiac and gastrointestinal problems," Dr. Carlin explained. "Standard reference sources and most available literature all list severe retardation, absence of speech and lack of ambulation as inevitable. But with the inception of early intervention programs, improved health, development and longevity have been demonstrated in a study of 62 individuals raised at home. Early intervention and a home setting are the keys to this improved outlook compared with the dismal predictions of the past."

At the next meeting in 1987, Dr. Joan Overhauser, author of a new study on the origin of Chromosome 5 deletions, was guest speaker along with Dr. Carlin. Talks by such noted medical professionals provide the opportunity to learn about the latest research.

"The very successes your children are now reaping because of your involvement and intervention are what is making the dire prognosis reported in the past obsolete," Dr. Carlin said.

She emphasizes how important it is to get the latest information out to dispel some of the dire stories given in the past, even by the medical community. Too many doctors are poorly informed. Since many children with birth defects used to be put in institutions with no stimulation or therapy, the prognosis was indeed bleak.

"The benefits of attending the annual get-together are obvious, but I brought back much more," one parent said. "We video taped the doctors' speeches as a good source for our group's library.

"What I didn't realize was how valuable the tapes could be to our five-year-old daughter's development. Her teachers and therapists viewed the tapes and reaction was remarkable."

"Since most articles written about 5p-Syndrome are outdated or negative, the only other information they had came from us. Now, there was a new degree of enthusiasm as the tapes helped them to better understand a child with the syndrome. Best of all, the teachers and therapists have correlated activities so that common goals can be obtained."

It was decided to move the location of the meeting each year to involve as many families as possible. Thirty families were at the sixth get-together in Pennsylvania in 1988 and 48 families met in Novi, Michigan, in 1989. The 1990 meeting was held in a dream location, Disney World in Orlando, Florida.

Parents also get practical information about infant stimulation, early childhood and public special education programs, physical, speech and occupational therapies at these get-togethers.

Farther down the road are loftier goals such as encouraging further research into prevention and early detection, studying ways to minimize the effects of resultant handicaps associated with the condition and techniques to maximize the child's development potential.

Members keep in touch all year through a quarterly newsletter that is a "place for all of us to meet and reach out to each other." Stories about individual children are shared as well as news, resources or techniques that have been especially helpful. Letters appearing in these newsletters from some of the parents speak volumes about the value of support groups.

"You could never know the impact that attending the Get-Together had on me," one mother wrote. "A lot of the parents I spoke with said they had waited four to five years to learn new information and be able to share their experiences. I waited for 14 years! My husband and I raised our son for 12 years without ever hearing about, let alone, seeing another child with this syndrome."

"My daughter is now 21 months old and is doing very well," another wrote. "But, it was hard for me and my family to cope with our "special child" because no one offered us any hope. One of the first things I was told was that she would be better off in a state home or hospital. Our daughter has shown me and everyone else that there *is* hope and whatever else anyone may say, being with the parents and lots of love is best. Thanks for the society because it helps me to be in touch with others for support."

These letters provide a personal look at how families discover, come to terms and cope with having a special child. Life with a handicapped child doesn't follow a set course, but sharing experiences help others cope and hope. Many support groups have periodic meetings and newsletters.

A newsletter by the Prader-Willi Syndrome Association helps parents share information with one another and provides professional advice as well. A recent issue reported on a Prader-Willi conference in Australia and reviewed data from Down Under.

"So many people don't know there is a place where they can get information and support," says Peter Bellerman, National Neurofibromatosis Foundation president, who estimates they have reached only 15 percent of those affected. Many of these non-profit organizations must do their own fund-raising since funds are not available from other sources.

REACHING OUT

Parent-to-Parent is a national program to provide support for parents of children with a range of disabilities. Under a variety of names this peer program provides support on a one-to-one basis with parents of newly diagnosed children. A "new" parent contacts the program to request help and is then matched primarily on the basis of the disabling condition.

Parents who form the experienced half of this match receive training to ensure their ability to handle emotional as well as information requests. Although there is no national Parent-to-Parent office, there are programs around the country.

"In Idaho, we didn't know anything for several years, that any research was being done, or that any information was available when our daughter was born in 1981," says Debra Johnson, Project Coordinator of Idaho Parents UnLimited, Inc., a federal training program. Since 1985, this statewide networking organization is dedicated to providing services for a full range of disabilities as well as promoting programs for parent training and developing support networks.

The fifth annual Parent-to-Parent conference in 1990 brought together parents of children with different disorders and ages at a national level. Participants had access to state-of-the-art resources as well as to professionals and policy makers. The first international gathering convened in 1992.

On the local level, Parent-to-Parent provides support and information with monthly meetings, peer counseling and newsletters. In Miami, Florida, there is an active support group with 50 chapters throughout the state and similar programs in many states.

"Our goal is to reach out and help each other and in so doing help ourselves," says Miami's president Paula Lalinde. In addition to the parent group meetings, there are also sibling and father support groups. Peer groups for siblings help them as much as support groups help the parents.

Raising a child with a disability presents many challenges, one of which concerns the relationship with siblings. Because of the problem, the handicapped child requires a large amount of family time. Equally important is the adjustment of the nondisabled child. According to the Barbara Walters unauthorized biography, she resented her mother's preoccupation with her retarded sister.

"Parents have to sit down and talk to the brothers and sisters who aren't handicapped and explain what the handicap means," advised one young sibling.

Some progressive hospitals and clinics have programs that include siblings and brings the entire family together. Presentations by "Kids on the Block" uses puppets to express feelings. At the Center for Family Studies in Morganstown, North Carolina, sisters and brothers take part in handicapped awareness exercises.

Various support groups include the issue of siblings at their meetings. Association of Children with Down Syndrome provides group support for siblings as well as fathers and grandparents. Hey, I'm Here Too! is a book published by the Muscular Dystrophy Association to help siblings of boys with Duchenne Muscular Dystrophy.

A statewide effort is underway in Florida to provide a clearinghouse for information on services for the disabled.

When the project is completed, a call to one phone number will tell where to find support groups, education and recreation programs, medical services and equipment, respite care, legal services and counseling.

Parent Education Network (PEN) offers training to help parents become effectively involved in the planning of their child's total education program. PEN and Parent to Parent merged in 1991 to become the Family Network on Disabilities. The new organization continues to provide local chapters with support, training materials and information.

A group of parents and professionals have collaborated in Dade County, Florida, since 1986 on a voluntary basis to ensure that special needs children from birth to five years and their families are provided with referral services. Through their efforts, model programs were created to include parent training, therapy and transportation services at no cost.

Project Thrive serves handicapped children from six weeks to three years with individualized speech and physical therapy and emphasizes parent training. Certified teachers provide infant stimulation in the home for those with such severe handicaps they are not able to attend a day program.

What started as a Pilot Parents Program in Omaha, Nebraska, became a four-state center and a national resource for information about Parent to Parent programs.

Patty McGill Smith, who was staff coordinator, moved from Omaha to Washington, D.C. to become Deputy Director of the National Information Center for Children and Youth with Handicaps, where she is a link of parent organizations nationwide.

She brings the personal perspective of a parent who knows what it's like to have a child with a handicapping condition.

"The day my child was diagnosed as having a handicap, I was devastated and so confused," she says.

She remembers the father of a retarded child who helped her. Twenty-two hours after her child's diagnosis, he made a

41

statement that she's never forgotten.

"You may not realize it today, but there may come a time in your life when you will find that having a daughter with a handicap is a blessing," he told her. She was puzzled by those words, but they offered her the first glimmer of hope for the future.

Her first recommendation is to try to find another parent of a handicapped child and seek assistance. The feeling of isolation at the time of diagnosis is almost universal among parents. These feelings can be diminished by realizing they have been experienced by many others, that constructive help is available, and above all that you are not alone. That help continues as members reach out to one another when new situations arise.

Wendy Bellack called members of her Parent to Parent support group of Broward County, Florida, for advice after she returned from Disney World with her six-year-old son.

"I thought it would be the all-American vacation." she said. "But, it was too much for him and he was overwhelmed. By talking with other parents, I realized many had experienced similar circumstances."

She was one of the original members who formed a chapter of the statewide organization in 1988. In addition to providing support, the group members help each other cope with education and plans for a child's adult years.

ADDENDUM

In response to her letter to Ann Landers, Melissa, the mother of an X-tra special boy with Klinefelter Syndrome, received over 1000 letters and was able to start a "kitchen table" support group.

Her letters came from every state and expressed almost universal feelings about the lack of medical and practical knowledge available on this syndrome, as well as the willingness to communicate and share concerns and successes with others who have the condition.

"After we received the diagnosis of our son's condition when he was seven, we were referred to a genetics clinic," Melissa said. "They had little information and could not put us in contact with anyone else who has K.S. It was amazing to us, given the fact that this is a common genetic disorder, that there was not more information readily available or that there was not a support group. This was the reason for our letter to Ann Landers."

SUPPORT GROUPS WORLDWIDE

The first International Gathering of Support Groups convened in Washington, D.C. on October 5, 1991. It marked the opening of formal communication between genetic support groups around the world.

Those attending the historic meeting agreed on the importance of forming an international alliance of support group networks to exchange ideas and information as well as to increase medical and public awareness.

Countries that made presentations were Australia, Hungary, India, Netherlands, Norway, Republic of South Africa and the United States. Other countries represented included Brazil, Canada, Dominican Republic, Israel, People's Republic of China, Taiwan, and Thailand.

Every parent of a special needs child and every affected individual feels the same kind of isolation, regardless of culture, tradition, or economic and social status.

All families worldwide have similar needs and hopes. By sharing the common experience, they can move from isolation to association.

An international alliance would provide a forum for mutual objectives. The first step has been taken to open channels of communication throughout the world.

CHAPTER 4

THEN AND NOW

Ask anyone whose baby was born with a birth defect over 25 years ago what was available and they'll tell you "hardly anything."

In the late 1960's and 1970's, a revolution in the care of the developmentally disabled took place. It was nationwide and supported by parents, government and providers of service resulting in significant improvements in medical treatment, education and opportunities.

Until that time it was believed people with mental retardation and other disabilities couldn't learn and were destined to a life of complete dependency. Many were placed in institutions and shut away from the rest of the world.

The earliest institutions for mentally retarded children in America began in the 1800's, but gradually only custodial care was provided and their low level functioning was seen as evidence they couldn't live in the community. Until recently, placement was recommended to parents as soon as the disability was diagnosed.

Systematic training efforts have clearly shown that even

those who are severely retarded can learn to care for their basic needs and adapt in many ways.

When her first baby was born in 1943, Anita J. of Milwaukee, Wisconsin, didn't know there was a problem although the birth was long and difficult. But, when her son rolled instead of crawled and didn't sit up, she knew something was wrong.

"My pediatrician was afraid to tell me," she recalls. "They really didn't know that much about cerebral palsy. I was advised to put him in an institution, but I couldn't do that."

"Finally someone told me where to get physical therapy at a clinic for handicapped children run by the Junior League. It was the best they had at the time. There was a total lack of facilities and understanding. Eventually he went to a school that accepted anyone with a physical handicap and when he was older, United Cerebral Palsy started a parents group that provided information and support. There is so much more available today."

Earlier in this century students of all ages were taught in a one room church-affiliated facility in Pennsylvania known as Home of the Merciful Savior for Crippled Children. Today, it is a school for students aged two to 20 with cerebral palsy.

During the early years of the St. Coletta Institute for Backward Youth (1904-1915), it was run by the Sisters of St. Frances of Assisi in Jefferson, Wisconsin. Today, the St. Coletta School provides programs for mentally retarded children and young adults.

The Devereaux Foundation started in 1912 with 12 students in a home-like atmosphere in Pennsylvania by Helena Devereaux, a pioneer of treatment programs for the developmentally impaired. It has grown to provide care for multi-handicapped and autistic as well, operating in 11 states.

The Anne Carlson School in Jamestown, North Dakota, originally served physically handicapped, but now has a large number of multi-handicapped children from several states. Children who would have died at birth years ago are living today at a new advanced care unit at the school, where children's medical needs are met along with therapy and education.

Since 1891, Children's Specialized Hospital in Mountainside, New Jersey, has been caring for children with special needs. Today, it is a comprehensive rehabilitation hospital for disabled children and recently added a long term care center for children requiring a total care environment.

Kluge Children's Rehabilitation Center at the University of Virginia Children's Medical Center has been caring for disabled children for 30 years and now uses a team concept for therapy and other procedures to provide coordinated care.

Care has come a long way in recent years. So has the public's attitude. Labels like backward, feeble-minded or imbecile were commonplace. Today, the bywords are special needs, handicapped or developmentally disabled.

By recognizing that a child between birth and school age has, or is at risk of having a handicapping condition or other special needs that affect development, early intervention is the means of providing services to lessen effects of the disability. Early intervention for infants and toddlers emphasizes basic skills such as crawling, pulling to stand, walking, using words and toys.

Research shows that early intervention using play techniques helps a child to learn. Lekotek Resource Centers began in Sweden where toys were adapted for children with disabilities. Translated from the Swedish word, play, the first American Lekotek opened in Evanston, Illinois, in 1980 and has expanded to over 50 centers in 19 states.

Thanks to early intervention from birth and quality education programs, along with a stimulating home environment and good medical care, children with handicapping conditions are being mainstreamed into society.

One of the first attempts at early intervention and therapies began 50 years ago at the Institutes for the Achievement of

Human Potential in Philadelphia, Pennsylvania. The treatment program initiated methods of crawling and patterning that are now in general use.

For over 20 years, the federal government has been supporting research into the effectiveness of early intervention. Results point conclusively that it is not only effective but can prevent the need for more services later in life.

LIFE EXPECTANCY

Spina bifida didn't require treatment years ago because all babies who had it died. Improved medical technology makes it possible to save many of these babies today. The 1990 March of Dimes poster child has spina bifida.

"Put phenobarbital in his bottle and wait for him to die," is what Dorothy and William Crawford, Sr. were told by doctors when their first child was born with spina bifida in 1950. Today, William Crawford, Jr. is a lawyer in Fort Lauderdale, Florida, who received the 1989 Florida Bar President Pro Bono Service award in recognition of his many hours of community service.

In the early 1900's, children with Down syndrome survived to a mean age of nine. With the discovery of antibiotics, they survived to about 20, and with advances in all aspects of clinical treatment, they now reach age 50 or older.

When the Cystic Fibrosis Foundation was established in 1955, few children with the fatal disease lived to start elementary school. Today, over half live beyond their mid 20's because of improved treatment.

Not only are these children living longer, but their quality of life has greatly improved as well.

When Chris Burke was born with Down syndrome in 1965, doctors told his parents he would probably never be able to feed and dress himself or read and write, and they recommended he be institutionalized. Putting their son in an institution was never an option for them. They took him home and through a slow process and good schooling, Chris became the successful young man he is today.

As the star of a TV show called, "Life Goes On," he plays a teen with Down syndrome. Only this actor is playing for real and is the first developmentally disabled actor in a TV series. The show attempts to eliminate stereotypes and introduce the public to a person with Down syndrome. Chris Burke was on the cover of Life Magazine in November, 1989, and is proof indeed that "Life Goes On."

A movie based on the autobiography of Christy Brown, born with cerebral palsy in Ireland in 1932, showed how he and his family coped with his disability. "My Left Foot" was nominated for an Academy Award in 1990 and Oscars went to the actor who played Brown and the actress who played his mother.

WHAT IS AVAILABLE NOW

New attitudes reflect fundamental changes in the lives of the disabled. A letter from President George Bush in Exceptional Parent magazine stated his commitment to citizens with disabilities and highlights the progress our country has made in integrating them into the mainstream.

In the past, severely impaired children got little help from the public sector. The Education for All Handicapped Children Act of 1975, changed that by giving disabled children access to public schools, assuring them a "free appropriate education" emphasizing special education and related services designed to meet their unique needs.

"Part of the law provides a tracking system so these children can be identified early," said Dr. Eleanor L. Levin, project director of Florida Diagnostic and Learning Resources

System. It defines "Handicapped children" as mentally retarded, hard of hearing, deaf, speech impaired, visually handicapped, orthopedically impaired or other health impaired, blind, multi-handicapped, specific learning disabilities or seriously emotionally disturbed.

In 1986, Congress recognized the importance of early intervention and mandated that school districts provide facilities and training for handicapped preschoolers by the 1990-91 school year. For children aged three to five and their parents this was very welcome news.

States are provided with money to prepare early intervention services for babies aged 0-two, who are developmentally delayed or at risk, and must obey federal regulations to participate in this program, which gives eligible children the right to services under the law. Although mandated in every state, it is difficult for families in rural areas to have access to all the services provided. ACRES, the American Council on Rural Special Education, serves as an advocate for rural special education and plans creative service delivery alternatives.

SPECIAL SCHOOLS FOR SPECIAL NEEDS

Some special schools around the country are under the auspices of organizations like the Association for Retarded Citizens, Easter Seal Society or United Cerebral Palsy and may be for specific conditions such as cerebral palsy, autism or Down syndrome.

An ARC developmental pre-school in Hallandale, Florida, has over 100 children with various disabilities, funded through HRS and the Department of Education. Children are placed in classrooms according to age and function level, receive speech, physical and occupational therapy and at five years of age go into cluster programs in special public schools.

The Quest School in Hollywood, Florida, was built in 1979 specifically for mentally and/or physically handicapped children aged five to 21. There are similar schools in many areas throughout the country.

The Debbie School, named after Debbie Segal who was born with cerebral palsy, provides early intervention for 0-2 years-old with separate programs for deaf and handicapped children. At three, they enter the Dade County, Florida, public school system. Ring-A-Round is an early intervention program for families with young handicapped children aged 0-7 sponsored by the Family Center of Nova University in Fort Lauderdale, Florida. Director of the Center is Dr. Marilyn Segal, a developmental psychologist specializing in early childhood, and the mother of Debbie Segal.

The goal of early placement in special schools is to mainstream as many children as possible into regular public school and eventually into society. Many children need therapy sessions daily to augment nursery, kindergarten and elementary school. Some are in self-contained classrooms with special education teachers, while others can go to regular public schools with aides.

A school to provide early intervention programs for infants, toddlers and pre-schoolers was started in 1973 by a group of parents who joined together to form the Association for Children with Down Syndrome in Bellmore, New York. Parents work in partnership with special education teachers as a team with speech, physical and occupational therapists, movements specialists, social workers and consultant pediatrician-geneticists.

Each child has an Individualized Education Plan designed by the team and parents are encouraged to participate. Current research shows that Down syndrome children benefit from early intervention programs. The infant and toddler program is for children from birth to five years, at which time they are referred to the local public school.

"Our baby was born with cerebral palsy and wasn't supposed to walk or talk," says Harvey Goodman of Fort Lauderdale, Florida. "Not only does she walk and talk, but she is now going to public school." Cassi Goodman went to the local United Cerebral Palsy school for children 18 months to five years until she could function elsewhere.

Her parents say that occupational, speech and physical therapies helped prepare her and "minimized the disability while maximizing the ability."

Physical therapy helps children develop gross motor skills such as crawling, walking, running and jumping. Babies may need help in head control or balance before they can learn to walk. Occupational therapy for young children improves fine motor skills using muscles of the arms, hands and face. Speech therapy benefits children with a language delay while alternative communication may be used if speech is impaired. These therapists work closely with parents to enhance their child's development. Sometimes state-of-the-art therapy is a combination of traditional and experimental methods. In the age of technology, toddlers work with computers at UCLA's Intervention Program for Handicapped Children.

When Lauren Hackland was born prematurely, the prognosis was extremely poor. She made such remarkable progress after starting rehabilitative therapy at nine months, that by two-and-a-half, she was selected as the 1990 Easter Seal Child for Dade County, Florida.

"She best represents what Easter Seals is all about," said Olga Villaverde from Easter Seal Society, which has helped disabled children and adults since 1942. Even occupational therapist, Laura Burke, who worked with her at the E.S. Rehabilitation Center, is amazed at her progress.

"When I started to work with her, she had no head control, couldn't use her eyes or roll over, and in less than two years, she learned to feed herself, use a walker and swim," she says.

The E.S.S. has a school for children with learning disorders along with an occupation, speech and therapy center, and in 1990 built a new $3.5 million school for 160 children to prepare them for the public school system.

Since 1975, when federal law first ensured access to schools, hundreds of thousands of children have received a better education alongside non-disabled peers. A school system more than half integrated is in Madison, Wisconsin, where disabled kids go to their home schools but share lunch, art and music with their non-disabled peers. Many schools have peer tutoring programs that allow disabled and non-disabled children to spend time together and develop friendships.

Not all special needs children can make it to a regular school environment. One teacher who works with the "profoundly mentally handicapped" children at an elementary school sees progress of a different kind.

"These children wither away if they don't get attention," says Algin Hurst, a finalist for 1990 Dade county Teacher of the Year. "That's what society traditionally did with these kids. Stick them in a corner and forget about them."

A doctor told the mother of one of his kids to put her son in a home because she wouldn't be able to care for him. Hurst says he already has been rewarded by getting the boy to be more independent and move around in his walker and hopes to get him walking soon.

Profoundly mentally handicapped is the bottom rung of the ladder, climbing to trainable, educable, emotionally handicapped and learning disabled. Different programs are available for many different handicapping conditions in many school systems.

Cathy Winecoff teaches the "educable mentally handicapped" at a public high school in Durham, North Carolina, in a model program for the transition from school to work.

"Our aim is to teach students to use a calculator and other survival skills needed in the outside world," says Winecoff, who helped write the proposal now in use.

53

The emphasis is on getting them ready to face the world at age 21, when public education stops. The purpose is to plug into other service agencies and expose the parents and child to what is available after school.

Depending on the handicapping condition, some may live in group homes or a complex with apartments specified for handicapped so they will eventually fit into the mainstream.

PARENTS GET INVOLVED

As part of the 1975 Education for the Handicapped Law, parent training information centers were created by the federal government. Most states have such projects to help parents become effectively involved in the planning, education and decision-making process for their child's total educational program.

The Parent Education Network of Florida is a training and information center for and by families of special needs children. Serving as an alliance of parents and professionals, support groups and service providers, PEN helps parents through Certified Trainers and workshops, newsletters and the latest news concerning education of handicapped children.

"We believe informed parents are effective parents," said PEN director Janet Jacob. "We have trained about 1,000 parents in workshops throughout the state since our group was formed in 1986." "We hope to do similar programs for the older child in the area of supported employment."

The mission of Parent Training Centers around the country is to assist parents. A recent survey revealed that 61 percent of parents knew nothing about their rights under the law.

"Our efforts are designed to help people with disabilities enter the economic mainstream through employment," said Robert Davila of the U.S. Office of Special Education and Rehabilitative Services. Nearly every state has Parent

Training and Information Centers.

The new generation of special needs children are better educated and more independent. As millions of these students graduate, they look ahead to employment.

One mother says it saves taxpayers money by bringing the disabled into the work force. She ignored physicians who urged to institutionalize her retarded son when he was born. Instead she kept him home and sent him to school with nondisabled children. At 18, he got a job in a stockroom and is a contributing member of society.

In the 1970's, special education students leaving the public school system were faced with entering a world of segregated dependency. In the 1980's, the emphasis shifted to early intervention, transition from school to work and family networking.

Cathy and Roger Cook worried about what would happen to their son, Caleb, who was born in 1978 with Down syndrome, if anything happened to them. They wanted him to be able to earn a living and care for himself in the future. With a family background in the restaurant business, they decided a bakery offering a variety of jobs at different levels would be an excellent training center for their son and others and leased a restaurant building in Groton, Connecticut.

"Many of the first student-workers couldn't speak, so teaching basic skills was our first order of business," Cathy said. "Job skills came later."

The non-reading students follow pictures to mix a cake batter, and others load a dishwasher. Teams at Seabird Bakery fill orders from local restaurants and eventually most move on to the retail operation or other private employment. For Caleb Cook and the other retarded children, the recipe for their future is much sweeter.

The 1990's will see more students with disabilities enter adult life in an integrated community setting. The transition from school to working life will enable them to participate in many aspects of society.

The focus for the nineties is the concept of independence for youth with special needs. As community schools, service agencies and employers advocate integrated life, Supported Employment will play a significant role in the future of the disabled. This type of program provides training and employment at various jobs in the community.

Many companies are already finding the disabled are very able workers. Pizza Huts is planning to hire 2,000 workers with disabilities over the next few years as part of their Jobs Plus Program. Their long term goal is to have two such workers in each of 700 stores and will restructure jobs to fit their special skills. Best of all, Pizza Hut is establishing business advisory councils in each state to urge other companies to set up similar programs. McJobs is McDonald's national program for employment of the disabled. Workers are trained by a job coach and placed in a store near their home where they receive competitive wages. Hardee's Food Systems hires employees with mental and physical disabilities through its "Capabilities" (Creatively Applying People's Abilities) program. Positions range from entry-level staff jobs to management.

A developmental training program for mentally retarded adults is sponsored by HRS and the United Way in Orlando, Florida. Primrose Center was established in 1952 to care for children not eligible for public school and later expanded to include adults who could benefit from prevocational training programs.

An Adult training program for ages 18 to 49 emphasizes social, self care and job related skills. An adult enrichment program for those over 50 offers enrichment in areas of daily living and leisure time skills.

Supported Employment places those with disabilities in community-based work sites under supervision. It enhances the quality of their life by providing meaningful work and at the same time provides reliable workers for the communities in three different counties.

Looking ahead to the 21st Century is a Parent Helping Parents group who met with professionals at a 1990 conference with a vision to create services for Californians with developmental disabilities in the year 2000.

"The theme that was repeated over and over was normalization, integration and choices," said Clare McDermott who attended the conference. "Many people were discussing the dissolution of state hospital systems in favor of community-based programs. The common ideal is to help those with disabilities live up to their potential and participate in the mainstream of life."

When doctors told Barbara and Bob Forrest to put their Down syndrome son in an institution they had another idea. Instead they started a multi-million dollar non-profit corporation that provides jobs and homes for mentally handicapped people.

The Carlsbad Association for Retarded Citizens in New Mexico began as a small sheltered workshop. Today, on an 85-acre farm, their son, Gary, and 120 others, earn paychecks working at businesses like a poultry operation producing 4,000 eggs a day, a 2,200-tree pecan grove or tend greenhouses. The recent purchase of a 5,000 acre ranch nearby added more jobs and a future summer campsite. Their country club neighbors have welcomed the 56 CARC residents, who live in seven ranch-style group homes.

"This isn't an institution," says Barbara Forrest, "it's a family."

LANDMARK LEGISLATION

The landmark Americans with Disabilities Act outlawed employment discrimination against the physically or mentally handicapped in 1990. Also, it requires businesses, telephone companies, bus and rail systems to make services accessible to the disabled.

The bill defines a disability as a condition that impairs "a major life activity," such as hearing, walking, seeing or working. It is the most important piece of civil rights legislation affecting people with disabilities since the Rehabilitation Act of 1973.

Former Connecticut Senator Lowell Weicker, who has a son with Down syndrome, introduced the first version of the act in 1988, and Iowa Senator Tom Harkin, who has a deaf brother, sponsored the revised bill. Ted Kennedy, who has a mentally retarded sister, is one of several lawmakers who backed the bill.

The aim of the bill is to get the handicapped out of state homes and institutions and into participation in society," says Senator Tom Harkin. "It will fundamentally change their lives."

New buildings will have to be made accessible to disabled people and employers must accommodate the physical needs of a disabled worker. Telephone companies will have to hire operators who can take a message typed by a deaf person on a Telecommunications Device for the Deaf (TDD).

This legislation has far reaching implications for state and local agencies to provide services and to the millions of disabled who can face the future with more hope than ever before.

Special education teachers are getting special training to help prepare graduating high school students to better participate in the workforce. They say only 15 percent got jobs above the minimum wage and are hopeful there will be more opportunities now.

"This bill will change my daughter's life," said the mother of a seven-year-old with cerebral palsy who walks with metal crutches. It will also change the lives for millions of others by focusing on abilities instead of disabilities and the promise of a brighter tomorrow. Enactment of the Americans with Disabilities Act means the present generation of special needs children can look forward to a future of greater participation in community life than ever before.

The Ten Commandments for Parents

1. Take one day at a time, and take that day positively. You don't have control over the future, but you do have control over today.

2. Never underestimate your child's potential. Allow him, encourage him, expect him to develop to the best of his abilities.

3. Find and allow positive mentors: parents and professionals who can share with you their experience advice and support.

4. Provide and be involved with the most appropriate educational and learning environments for your child from infancy on.

5. Keep in mind the feelings and needs of your spouse and your other children. Remind them that this child does not get more of your love just because he may get more of your time.

6. Answer only to your conscience; then you'll be able to answer to your child. You need not justify your actions to your friends or the public.

7. Be honest with your feelings. You can't be a super-parent 24 hours a day. Allow yourself jealousy, anger, pity, frustration, and depression in small amounts whenever necessary.

8. Be kind to yourself. Don't focus continually on what needs to be done. Remember to look at what you have accomplished.

9. Stop and smell the roses. Take advantage of the fact that you have gained a special appreciation for the little miracles in life that others take for granted.

10. Keep and use a sense of humor. Cracking up with laughter can keep you from cracking up from stress.

From a Parent Group

CHAPTER 5

SPECIAL CHILDREN, SPECIAL FAMILIES

It is never easy to find out your child has "special needs." For it is also the family that must cope and deal with the special changes in all their lives.

"There must be acceptance and the knowledge that sorrow fully accepted brings its own gifts," wrote Pearl S. Buck in "The Child Who Never Grew." For there is alchemy in sorrow. It can be transmuted into wisdom, which, if it does not bring joy, can yet bring happiness."

The author, who won the Nobel Prize for literature, said she learned a lesson for dealing with life's problems by raising a child with mental retardation.

Many others who are faced with raising a special needs child say that we may not have control over what comes our way, but we can choose how we respond.

Here are some of those families and their personal responses.

CHASE BLAKE'S STORY

Chase Blake looks like most other four-year-old boys as he bites into a hot dog at lunchtime. What makes him different is that he takes four pills with everything he eats to help him digest a meal and a total of 40 pills a day. Chase has cystic fibrosis. It affects his digestive system as well as his lungs. After lunch, he has one of three treatments he needs every day.

At this session, respiratory therapist Nathan Winton pounds his back to break up the thick mucus that could choke him. It is this mucus in the lungs that produces the bacterial infections that can cause death to the victim by the average age of 27.

He also has to use an aerosol breathing device with medication to open his airwaves as part of his daily therapy. The therapist does two treatments, while mom or dad do the other. Until Chase was 18 months old, his parents did them all. The treatments cost $120 a day, 365 days a year.

"These lung treatments are part of his life," says Nathan. "He's accepted it. It's easier when it's started young."

"It's my life, too," says Natalie, Chase's mother. "Our lives are not normal," she adds. "We know Nathan is coming to do the treatment."

But life settles into a routine and Chase started going to a normal playschool when he was three-and-a-half. His parents worry about him picking up an infection, which quite often leads to pneumonia in those with cystic fibrosis.

"We are making our life as normal as possible," says Natalie. "Being active is best for these kids since it moves the mucus around."

"I don't look at him as someone who's going to die. I want him to live his life to the fullest. You have to live like you're going to live. He gets so much out of life."

"Mommy, why do I have cystic fibrosis?" Chase asked recently. "Because you were born with it," was her reply.

Chase was two months premature and weighed only three pounds, four ounces at birth. He was diagnosed with CF and on top of that, his lungs weren't fully developed.

"I did not become attached to him in the beginning because I was afraid he was going to die", admits Natalie. "I never went home from the hospital with a baby," she said. "My first child, Ian, was born with his bladder outside his body and had the first of many surgeries when he was 16 hours old."

The genetic counselor said it was not genetic, but a fluke of nature. Just to rule out the problem, Natalie had a sonogram when she was 29 weeks pregnant with Chase and knew there was a blockage in his intestine, but not what it meant.

Like many others, they entered a new world that changed their lives forever. She remembers a psychiatrist at the time telling her, "You were given lemons. Now make lemonade."

"It makes you appreciate what is important," Natalie says. "The good times are very good and the bad times are very bad but I get a lot of strength from my children."

Friends don't treat them differently and the boys rough-house like other brothers. They all try to live as normally as possible within the restraints of the condition.

They joined a CF support group of local parents in the area and were surprised to find six families in a two mile area. Not only do they interact with other parents but also get valuable information, such as finding the Home Health Service which provides medication and therapy.

"I feel he will be cured," said Nathan, his respiratory therapist. "It will be a while, but there is great hope."

The reason for this optimism is the 1989 discovery of the cystic fibrosis gene, which can lead to treatment for children like Chase.

"We can finally look in the eyes of children and young adults with Cystic Fibrosis and tell them that the door to their future has been opened," said CFF President Robert K. Dresing, whose 22-year-old son has cystic fibrosis.

HEATHER'S STORY

Perhaps 11-year-old Heather's story is best told by her brother and sister. "She hugs and kisses a lot and she plays with me a lot," says four-year-old Rebecca. "We don't care if she can't play Nintendo. It's just a game. We care about real life." (Out of the mouths of babes.)

"I don't care that she's retarded," says Adam, who is 18 months younger than Heather. "She's just slower and can't really talk, but I can play with her. She doesn't cause much trouble at all."

"Heather wanted to do everything he did," says Mom Eileen Sherman. "It was good for her because it pushed her to do things. When he got old enough to understand, he became her defender."

Heather was born with Cri-du-chat, a chromosomal disorder that causes mental retardation and other disabilities. But this family isn't letting it stop them at all. Like most other families raising a child with a disability, they reached out for support. They found it in a group for their daughter's specific condition as well as a local group for various disabilities.

In 1982, five Chicago parents met to discuss the difficulties of raising their special needs children. They shared problems at home and in the community. A lack of communal awareness and difficulty in finding services for their children motivated them to start a new organization, Keshet. It has grown to over 200 families in the Chicago area. Monthly parent group meetings provide a network of support and information. Each month a special group is conducted for brothers and sisters of handicapped children to explore issues of growing up with a disabled sibling. A parent-to-parent

Special Children, Special Families

hotline is available to discuss concerns or sometimes "just to talk."

One of the original founders of Keshet went one step further. Marcia Routberg and Social Worker Seena Platt organized Parent Consultants to provide workshops and seminars for parents of special children.

A DOUBLE STORY

Looking at Kerrie and Kacie Grady, adorable nine-year-old twin girls, it's hard to realize one of them suffers from a serious birth defect.

"They didn't look too much alike at birth because one had dark hair and the other had none," remarked Sandy Grady, mother of the fraternal twins, who were born minutes apart before and after midnight so their birthdays are on two different days.

Their pediatrician noticed other differences and by the time they were less than a year old he told the shocked parents he thought Kacie had neurofibromatosis, a big word for a little girl.

"Another doctor confirmed his opinion," Sandy said. "I found out the grim prognosis that means tumors and the lifelong fear that it can get much worse. It is a time bomb."

NF affects people differently and is unpredictable, often causing disfigurement, paralysis, and can lead to death.

For Sandy, who has a PhD in education, she wanted to know more about the disease and what it all meant. She learned it affects one in 4,000 and in 50 percent it is a spontaneous mutation, as with Kacie.

"There were no books, no NF listing in the phone book," she recalled. "I called all over to get information and became an NF volunteer."

It was in that role that she played a part in helping to

isolate the NF gene. Nobody had enough families to get blood samples to examine. She met a newly diagnosed man with a very large family and doctors drew 130 blood samples for chromosome comparisons. Blood samples provide clues to solving genetic mysteries.

The twins were seven years old the year the NF gene was discovered in 1989. Sandy has learned a lot in the intervening years since Kacie was diagnosed.

"The reality is a jolt," she says. "In one moment, all my dreams for the twins changed from high school graduation to a double wedding. I needed to find the strength not to let the pain overcome us."

' "I had a three-year-old daughter when the twins were born and she had to grow up very quickly. The parents, siblings and the affected child all relate differently."

"When I was younger, I didn't really understand and I was a bit jealous of the attention Kacie got," admits 11-year-old Katherine. "As I began to understand what it was all about, I realized why my Mom was so upset and worried about her."

"I'm glad Kacie doesn't have any tumors now and maybe she can live a normal life," she said hopefully. "I think she will be cured."

"Kerrie, the unaffected twin, wants to know why it happened to her sister and not to her," says Sandy. "Her pain is just as real."

"My husband and I both changed jobs because the most important thing was to get group medical coverage. We didn't have the luxury of waiting."

Now the Grady family is waiting for the most important news of all – that there is treatment to prevent NF's progression or a cure.

A DIFFERENT STORY

For Aileen Ross, there was a side of her that wanted her children to live at home. But her other side knew it was better for them to be at Miami's Hope Center and come home for week-ends and holidays.

"I wish I could be with my children as a regular family," says the divorced mother of two retarded children, "but I realize they have a social life there and can do things with other kids that I couldn't provide for them."

"It is really the best of both worlds. During the week, they have their peers and activities, and when they come home it is special.

"They cannot read or write, so they are limited in what they can do," she explains. "They are trainable and can learn vocational skills, although they probably will never live alone.

"Like all teenagers, they enjoy music, good food and parties. The most uncomfortable thing is what other people do to us when they stare. Most retarded people are very social and want social acceptance. They have their own interactions, make friends and get crushes."

"It is painful to realize there will be no graduations, no weddings, no grandchildren," she says. "But, you learn to accept the situation and go on from there."

For Marge Stack, the decision to look for an alternative for her 17-year-old daughter came because she felt it would be better for the entire family. Through HRS, Michelle was accepted into a group home that is only ten minutes away from the family home.

"It's still hard at times," Marge admits. "But, it has made a difference in our lives. I haven't relinquished custody and I can see her every day."

"I bring her home as often as I can," says Marge, who works at the same public school that her daughter attends for the mentally/physically handicapped. "Now when she's home, I have more patience. I feel good about it. She's doing well at the group home and has friends there. My normal 15-year-old son was always being pushed aside because I was so busy with her. Now I have extra time for him."

"She's still our daughter and when she gets sick, she comes home and I take care of her. We have her with us for all the major holidays and recently took her to Disney World and had a great time. It's working out well for us all."

A MOTHER'S STORY

DREAMS OF MOTHERHOOD
by Wendy Bellack

Before I had children, I used to dream about motherhood. I had such visions of what it would be like. I would not return to the work place like so many Moms must do, I would stay at home and be the "perfect Mom".

It has been almost eight years since I got married and I now have two beautiful children. My son is 6 1/2 years old and my daughter just about to turn five. This certainly looks like the "All-American family". This was one of the times I used to dream about. With diapers, bottles and schedules behind us, this was going to be the time for all of those wonderful family outings I had planned. The zoo, the circus, the library, learning to ride a bike, holiday shopping and baking were all going to be experiences that created family memories. Oh, what dreams I had. Instead of being enjoyable, these activities can sometimes become nightmares. My son has a disability known as Pervasive Developmental Disorder. His reactions and behaviors can be very unpredictable and even when my husband and I think we have planned extensively and covered all bases, things don't always work out.

But in the past six years we have certainly learned a great deal. Not only have we learned about children with disabilities but we have learned a lot about life. We have learned not to expect every situation to turn out "picture perfect". We have learned to be more flexible and we have learned not to set ourselves up for disappointment. We have also learned to laugh again.

I won't say that any of this came easy. But I can say, that now that we have gotten past all that we are enjoying ourselves again. We enjoy our children and we cherish their moments of achievement. Even though Steven's accomplishments are the result of countless hours of practice, Jill's development is just as precious to us. We are sensitive to her needs and indulge her without spoiling. Sometimes, when I accompany her to a birthday party or a trip to the mall, I can picture myself in my dreams of long ago. I have learned that these special "dates" are healthy for both of us. It is but a temporary escape and an opportunity to give Jill my undivided attention. When we are at home things are usually more hectic and Steven requires more supervision and direction. Our special time together is limited but we learn together. We cannot afford to miss a chance at improving our communication skills. Even our "snuggle time" is a time to talk about feelings and emotions. Hugging and kissing is something that Steven enjoys and it's so much fun.

I thought that being a full-time mother would be a breeze. But there is so much more to this than cooking, cleaning, ironing, loving and hugging. Having a child with "special needs" has given motherhood a whole new meaning. I never dreamed it could change my life so much. I had planned to teach my children so much and I have, but they have taught me a great deal more.

THE OTHER STORY

Not every story means a child will be at the top end of achievement. Some will be at the lower end. Not every child with Down syndrome will be like the boy depicted on TV's "Life Goes On."

These children will never be on TV or have stories written about them or their successes. But special parents of these special children say they accept the realities of limited abilities and along with their child enjoy the simple pleasures of life. Their stories are about a different kind of success.

Those feelings are expressed in a poem written by a father to his Special Boy:

Hey there, you character with a smile on your face,
You seem the most happy of the whole human race.
Like any boy, you romp and play,
Unlike most children, that's the way you'll stay.
You laugh and cry like other boys,
And never grow tired of your many toys.
You are a joy to Mother and me,
Because you're a special boy, you see.

GRANDPARENTS ARE SPECIAL, TOO

An extended family is important to everyone, but with a special needs child, it proves a safe haven.

"Grandparents are a safety net," said Gene LaRue, a special grandparent of a special needs baby. "We can help ease the burden and help care for them."

The special education teacher admits it wasn't easy for the family to adjust.

"After saying Why Me?, I said why not me?" explains LaRue, who teaches vocational education to handicapped adults. "I've got a 25-year background in special ed with a major in learning disabilities.

"We stick together as a family and do the best we can," he adds. "It is our four-year old grandson who motivates us."

His son and daughter-in-law found out there was a problem when their baby was three months old. When he was four months old, they signed papers and gave him up for adoption. At 10 months, the foster parents were in the process of adopting Zachary, but, his mother and father decided they wanted him back and prevailed.

"I'm so glad we got him back," says LaRue. "I'd bring him to my house week-ends in the beginning, but now he lives full-time with me temporarily. We're keeping him so his parents can finish school. It's hard, but I love him."

His son had a good job but decided to go to law school so he can give Zachary a secure future. His daughter-in-law is in pre-med and is applying to medical school as a result of her child's condition. She wants to become a geneticist.

Margaret Johnson is the grandmother of three-year-old Jared McDaniels and thinks having a special needs child is a good example to us that life is like a road with a few bumps along the way.

"I'm so fortunate to have such a lovely grandchild," she said proudly. "I think he's beautiful. He likes music and is always very loving."

"She's a part of me," says a Chicago grandmother. "We just accept her and love her. We've all learned to work with her disability."

A Texas grandmother with 27 grandchildren admits she loves her "special" three-year-old grandson best of all. The first few months were very difficult for everyone, but the family says it's smooth sailing now and they wouldn't give him up for the world.

The grandmother of a little girl born with cystic fibrosis lives far away from her. But that didn't stop this determined grandmother from starting a CF chapter in her hometown. She became very involved and encouraged her friends to support charity events to raise money for research.

At a recent national support group meeting, several grandparents were very involved. Some came with their children and grandchild. One set of grandparents came instead of their son and daughter-in-law who couldn't make it.

Martha Suter of Kansas came with her parents and two-year-old son, Justin. Her husband suffers from serious kidney disease and had to stay home.

"We're glad to help all we can in a doubly difficult situation," said Justin's grandfather. "He requires a lot more care than a normal child. We take it one day at a time. We know we will spend the rest of our lives caring for him because his mom has to work and with his dad's medical problem, we do what we have to do."

"He's so precious and does things we didn't expect," says his grandmother. "The literature we got from the doctor was from the dark ages. He is doing so much more than what they told us when he was born. He is crawling, pulling up and trying to walk around. I could go on all day about him. He has been such a blessing for us. We love him so much. He is a very special little boy," says this very special grandmother.

Grandparents, aunts, uncles, siblings, cousins and a myriad of other relatives help make raising a special needs child just a little easier.

CHAPTER 6

AT HOME OR
HOME AWAY FROM HOME

As little as 20 years ago, the residential institution was the
norm and the only service available for parents who couldn't
deal with their child's disability alone. Today, the trend is
away from institutions with community-based care providing
alternatives and a wide range of living options.

Some parents look for residential programs when they feel
around-the-clock trained staff will help their child reach
maximum potential. There are many residential schools
throughout the country providing stimulation and educational
services where parents can be as involved as they want to be.

A Bill of Rights of Retarded Persons was enacted by the
federal government in 1975 declaring that the system of care
which the states provide must be designed to meet the needs
of retarded persons.

The main goal was to continue the development of community-based services as alternatives to institutionalization and to
provide education and training as well.

Each client or parent receives a copy of this act from the

state Department of Health and Rehabilitative Services and each residential facility is required to post a copy of the regulations, all aimed at promoting the best interests of its residents.

Since its establishment in 1955, Hope Center in Miami, Florida, grew from six students to a broad-based organization serving 120 residents who vary in levels of retardation. Each person is placed in an appropriate homelike setting.

"When my son was born 40 years ago, there were no answers to our questions," said Dr. Judy Holland, Hope Center's executive director. "Worse than that, most available places were a nightmare. That is why the Hope Center was born."

"Our main focus is on residential services and community-based employment," she says. "Our goal is to enrich their lives by helping them relate to the society in which they live and to achieve their full potential."

The dorm residence program is the most supervised, while other living arrangements include a half-way house for those 18 years or older who are able to function semi-independently. It is, as the name implies, a way to prepare them for independent living without putting them out on the street before they are ready.

The basic ingredients of the academic program are special education and "normalization" classes. Survival education is also emphasized to further enable 'graduates' to function as independently as possible in the community. To continue the educational process, pre-vocational and vocational programs are designed to encourage proper work skills and career awareness.

At the Independent Living Unit, residents are totally responsible for their own care and personal duties, with an apartment supervisor nearby. They live in an apartment complex and work either at Hope Center or other locations in the area. They handle their own personal duties including banking and using public transportation. Some work in supermarkets, restaurants or at clerical duties such as in the District Attorney's office. One group decided to take a three-day cruise with the money they earned.

Skills are taught at a vocational workshop and employs those unable to work in the private sector who fill work contracts that include assembling, packaging and bulk mailing.

Looking ahead to the future, a new state-of-the-art vocational rehabilitation center will provide an expanded training program to fill more jobs from the local community with workers proving to be dependable employees.

The Hope Center motto says it all – where there is love, there is HOPE. By progressive programs, the developmentally disabled can remain with sheltered supervision or move out into the community.

Aileen Ross moved from California to Florida in 1980 when she was looking for the right environment for her two children. She says she found it at the Hope Center, where she works as director of development.

"About 80 percent of our clients are recipients of HRS and receive an average of $600 a month," she said. "Since it cost $2,500 per person per month, there is a $1,900 shortfall that must be made up by direct donations, grants and fund raising. The other 20 percent of clients are private and pay on a sliding scale."

"Three hots and a cot is the slang expression for what we have to provide," she adds. "But, at Hope Center there are so many extra services that we must make up the difference."

"Hope Center is one of the few places that lets you keep your child weekends or spend time with their family," she says.

The former audio and speech pathologist was unprepared when her first child was diagnosed as mentally retarded. Doctors couldn't find a genetic basis, so she had another child, who also is mentally retarded.

"At that time, people put their children away or kept them

hidden at home," she says. "Awareness of mental retardation was very limited before the era of the Kennedys."

In 1946, Joseph Kennedy established the Joseph P. Kennedy Jr. Foundation named after his late son, to help the retarded. The family's interest stems from daughter, Rosemary, who was born retarded.

Over 100,000 babies are born in the United States each year with mental retardation and seven million Americans are mentally retarded.

The Berkshire Children's Community in Great Barrington, Massachusetts, is a private residential school for moderately, severely and profoundly retarded children from early infancy to age 21, who may also have other handicaps.

The program is a model for bringing retarded young people to their level of independence. Regardless of skill level, the emphasis is on growth. The profoundly retarded and severely physical handicapped children live in a home that has been structurally modified and equipped. Those who have made substantial progress live in special needs foster homes in nearby communities as preparation for a more independent setting in the future.

A facility for developmentally disabled children and adults with severe/profound mental retardation is Sunrise Community for the Retarded which serves 350 in Connecticut and Florida with no age restrictions.

A variety of residences run the gamut from cluster homes providing medical care to group homes promoting greater independence. The surroundings are made as homelike as possible and appropriate for individual needs.

In the late 1950's, five parents of children with mental retardation and other developmental delays wanted an alternative to state-run institutions and in 1959, they pooled their resources and built three cottages in Palatine, Illinois. Today, Little City is a training and residential facility on a 56-acre campus.

Pathfinder Village in Edmeston, New York, is a residential center exclusively for Down syndrome and is home to 82 children and adults.

"No longer are Down syndrome people raised behind a fence, segregated and treated differently," says Marian Mullet, chief executive officer of Pathfinder, which was established in 1980.

Here, older children with Down syndrome get "hands on" experience working in local establishments. They leave their classes to learn real work skills at jobs in a day care center, bakery, general store, restaurant or public library in the community.

It's not all work and no play as the children participate in sports and many go to summer camp. A new gymnasium and sports center is scheduled for completion in 1992. The biggest project is yet to come. A comprehensive Information and Resource Center on Down Syndrome is proposed for 1995 for parents and professionals from all over the world.

Since 1983, The Anne Carlsen School in North Dakota provides residential care for moderately to severely disabled students along with education and rehabilitation therapy. Their goal is to integrate the child back into the home as soon as possible.

The Devereaux Foundation was founded in 1912 by Helena Devereaux, who recognized the need of special people to feel useful and established learning opportunities that were not available by traditional systems.

Today, it is a nationwide organization that operates residential and day treatment facilities for those with a wide range of developmental and neurological disorders. Although headquartered in Devon, Pennsylvania, it serves over 2,000 children and adults in 11 states. Some locations are specifically for mentally retarded and/or developmentally disabled, autistic, hearing impaired, learning disabled, Prader-Willi Syndrome, Tourette Syndrome or dual diagnoses.

Originally, the treatment program for brain-injured children at the Institutes for the Achievement of Human Potential in Philadelphia was on an in-patient basis. As staff and parents worked together over the years, they discovered that a home treatment program produced even better results. Today, the focus is on developing and teaching treatment programs to parents for use at home. On one Monday of every month, a group of parents and their children arrive at the Institute to learn these methods.

The Institute of Logopedics in Wichita, Kansas, provides a residential school for students with multiple handicaps and communication disorders (logopedics means the study and treatment of speech disorders.) A heavy emphasis is on speech and communication to help develop functional communication skills.

The familiar refrain of My Old Kentucky Home has applied to the Stewart family since 1983, when they started a home and school for the mentally retarded. Over the years the physical facilities and staff have grown, and today, Dr. John P. Stewart is the resident physician, overseeing this home away from home.

The HMS School for Children originally named Home of the Merciful Savior for Crippled Children was founded in 1882 as a charitable organization. Today it is a school for children with cerebral palsy in Philadelphia, and offers a total habilitation of residential and therapy programs for children from two to 20.

Elwyn has grown from a small, private school in Pennsylvania that now serves 8,000 handicapped children and adults at 40 separate locations in four states. New training programs allow many individuals to work at job sites in the community with follow-up support by the staff.

Keystone Training and Rehabilitation Residence in Scranton, Pennsylvania, established in 1964, was a pioneer in the concept of an urban based rehabilitation and residential facility for the mentally retarded. Today, a multistage living arrangement is offered with an open door policy so family and friends may visit at any time.

In 1957, the parents of an 11 year-old blind and mentally retarded girl searched for a school that could help her and found there simply weren't any. Her parents were determined to give their daughter, Judy, the care she needed. Dr. Charles Jordan and his wife, Mary, of Springfield, Illinois, founded the Hope School to train Judy and other blind and multi-handicapped children who had no place to go.

The Hope School had its beginning in an old six-room house and today is a residential school for 108 multi-handicapped children and adults between the ages of three and 18 who come from all over the United States. Only their policy has remained the same – of accepting only those children who have been rejected by other schools.

A residential community for mentally retarded adults was begun by a group of concerned parents in 1966 with a vision of something better for their children. As an alternative to placement in a large institution or traditional community based group home, the New England Villages provides residential options in a family environment for retarded adults 18 years or older. Each residence houses 4 to 8 people along with a professional trained staff, and some achieve independent living. Parents continue to be very involved.

Ellen and Myer Savits searched for the right residential facility for their mildly retarded son and found few existed that met their particular requirements or the waiting period was too long. So they decided to open their own place for their 30-year-old son and others desiring a semi-independent environment. Ellen, a social worker, and Myer, a music professor, have both specialized in working with the retarded and developed a therapeutic program in conjunction with regular services. Their son, who was born brain damaged and retarded, has worked for several years in a brokerage firm doing clerical jobs.

Some families turn to Catholic, Jewish or other religious family services. Many communities have residential schools or other programs.

"Today, parents are less afraid to acknowledge they have a retarded child and may need support or placement," said Lester Kaufman, Executive Director of Ohel Children's Home and Family Services in Brooklyn, New York.

Responding to the needs in the Jewish community, it was founded in 1970 and has grown to encompass an extensive system of residential and outpatient treatment facilities for disabled children as well as adults and their families.

In 1982, five parents in the Chicago area met to discuss raising their special needs children who had various disabilities. Although the conditions of the children were different, problems in the home and community were similar. They realized that as a group, they could initiate needed programs and activities. The organization is called Keshet, the Hebrew word for rainbow symbolizing the promise of hope, and has grown to over 200 families. Few residential facilities were available and a major goal was reached with the establishment of a Keshet group home for mildly involved adults.

St. Coletta's School in Wisconsin was founded in 1904 and is now a year-round academic residential program for mentally retarded children and young adults from six to 25. It also provides habilitation and vocational training with community transitional group homes.

This is just a small sampling of various types of facilities. According to the Association of Retarded Citizens, there are over 16,000 residential facilities in the United States today, whose goal is to allow greater numbers of people with mental retardation to live in group homes.

EMPHASIS ON INDEPENDENT LIVING

The wave of the future is group homes as part of the trend against institutions for the mentally and physically disabled. Group homes are houses in residential areas where six to eight people live with one or more care givers and have become more widely used in the last decade, offering a chance for self-reliance.

Some group homes are designated to serve only those with a specific handicap, such as Down Syndrome or Prader-Willi Syndrome, to concentrate on specific needs. Parents open band together to take on the project themselves.

"Very seldom does a state step forward and open a facility for us," say Marge A. Wett, executive director of Prader-Willi Syndrome Association. "A greater percentage of the time it is a group of parents taking a great deal of effort to get the county and state to approve."

But, the work does pay off and there are now Prader-Willi homes in Delaware, New York, Maryland, Illinois, Pennsylvania, Missouri, Indiana and Michigan and a children's home in California.

"Our concern for the future of our children motivates us to find alternate living arrangements," says Rosella Van Swearingen, who tried to get a group home in her area. With help from HRS and UCP, funding was made available to build a group home in Fort Lauderdale, Florida.

The state of California licenses special foster care homes for developmentally disabled children. The theory is to keep children out of institutions and in a homelike setting. Placement is paid for by the state and social services, with parents paying a contribution based on income. Parents retain custody and can be as involved with their children as they want.

For those special needs children raised at home, parents

have many more options available today than every before.
The independent living movement has flourished by teaching
and encouraging severely disabled people to live more
independently within their homes and community. Data
suggests it is less costly for people with disabilities to live in
the community than an institution.

A landmark survey of in-home support services in all 50
states by the World Institute on Disability provided a first step
in establishing guidelines for necessary service programs.

"Parents are a child's strongest advocate," says occupational
therapist Louella Miller. Her advice to parents is to be an
informed consumer of services.

INDEPENDENT LIVING CENTERS

Over 200 Independent Living Centers have opened since
the 1970's, offering various support services to the disabled
and enabling them to fit more easily into society by helping
them achieve productive lives in their own community. The
centers are usually non-residential and controlled by people
with disabilities to provide independent living skills training,
peer counseling and information.

Independent Living Centers developed out of a need for
people with disabilities to have more control over their lives.
A lack of barrier-free housing and classroom buildings at the
University of California at Berkeley prompted a severely
disabled student to join with other disabled students and form
one of the first centers in the country. Within a short time,
disabled students from all over began to move to the Berkeley
area because now there was a place with programs and
services for them.

In the nearly two decades they have been in existence, the
ILC's have taught people to handle their own finances,
manage self-care, travel without assistance and enroll in

appropriate education or job-training programs. They are now referred to ILC's by schools, hospitals and advocacy organizations.

Centers for rehabilitation and research are springing up across many university campuses, such as The Center for Rehabilitation Technology at Georgia Tech where experiments with new technologies help people with severe disabilities better adapt to their environment.

One of the chief aims of The Technology-Related Assistance for individuals with Disabilities Act of 1988 is to provide federal assistance to states to develop programs of "consumer responsive" assistive technology services. It has been found that people with disabilities benefit most when they or their families have played an informed and vital role in assessing and selecting the assistive technology.

Many disabled people don't know about new technologies that can help them or where to get special information about special equipment.

The computer age reaches into the world of the disabled and offers independence, employment and information, allowing some people to work at home, communicate without being able to speak and read without being able to turn the pages. Many organizations are helping the handicapped gain access to computer-related technology.

Rapidly changing technology and the growth of independent living centers has generated the need for access to a wide range of information, and in 1977 The National Rehabilitation Information Center (NARIC) was established. Fifty percent of the staff are themselves disabled and all of the staff are professionals with backgrounds in disability-related fields and information dissemination.

The National Council on Independent Living (NCIL) is a membership association of Independent Living Centers founded in 1982. Many of the centers have utilized NARIC's information on adaptive equipment and the relationship is

83

growing as more centers discover available resources.

The National Parent Network on Disabilities is a new coalition of parent organizations to provide a national voice for parents of children with disabilities. By sharing information and resources they hope to influence and effect policy issues concerning the needs of those with disabilities and their families.

The NPND covers the whole range of disabilities and can provide a strong advocacy voice to communicate needs and priorities and is a link between parent organizations to share their expertise.

Areas of concern change as the special needs child gets older and go from coping with the disability to planning for the future. This includes career plans, placement, wills and guardianship and many support groups provide access to information.

The Association of Retarded Citizens is setting up a national program to assist with a variety of issues including medical and life insurance.

RESPITE CARE

As increasing numbers of children with disabilities are kept at home, there is an increasing need of respite for their parents. The word respite means "relief by an interval of rest."

Caring for a child with disabilities can be a full-time job. In the past, many parents with special needs children hesitated to ask for relief because their child required special care.

Now respite provides support for parents by giving them time away from the care of their youngsters. Respite workers receive training in understanding developmental disabilities and in caring for a child with special needs.

New federal legislation recognized this very real need by

voting on Temporary Child Care for Handicapped Children in 1989 and many local organizations and agencies are providing it or have information on respite care services in most communities. Over 30 states have passed legislation for in-home family support systems, including respite care.

United Cerebral Palsy has an in-home respite program for developmentally disabled children from birth to 18 years. The Association for Retarded Citizens, with over 1,300 chapters in the United States, can make referrals for short term respite care. Hermann's Children's Hospital in Houston, Texas, opened Respite House so parents have free time while the staff looks after the children.

The National Down Syndrome Society created Project Child, a model independence respite program that gives children aged five to 12 a chance to visit volunteer families on weekends. It is a symbiotic relationship and gives the community positive attitudes toward those with Down Syndrome as volunteer families "adopt" a child for a weekend.

"Fifteen years ago, these children might have been institutionalized," said one of the parents. "Now, a safe environment is provided for our children to interact with others and learn social skills." NDSS has been awarded a grant to establish the program throughout the country. In some areas, ARC, in conjunction with a local Down Syndrome group, has instituted this respite program. Local agencies and organizations have information on respite care services in most communities as well as special departments in area schools.

TIME FOR PLAY

Summer camp programs offer a respite resource for families of children with disabilities. Many are accredited by the American Camp Association and are located throughout the country. Some are for children with mental retardation, multiple handicaps, or for specific conditions.

Muscular Dystrophy of America provides summer camping activities geared to the special needs of those with neuromuscular diseases aged six to 21. In 1989, MDA sponsored 110 camp sessions in 44 states and Puerto Rico, staffed by volunteer physicians and nurses. Each camper has a volunteer counselor, who is usually a high school or college student.

A variety of programs are available around the country. Therapy and the Performing Arts has been established in the Boston area to allow children and young adults to participate free of charge. Classes are taught by certified instructors in music, dance, drama and art, along with skiing, ice-skating and horseback riding. Several Kiwanis clubs sponsor free riding programs to handicapped youngsters with some competing in special horse shows each year. Many organized programs are dedicated to helping the handicapped with therapeutic horseback riding. A young rider from Hozhoni Riding Center in Durango, Colorado, won a gold medal at Special Olympics. The North American Riding for the Handicapped Association has a list of accredited programs.

In some areas, playgrounds are specially equipped for special needs children. They are designed to accommodate children with and without a disability by having elevated sandboxes, wheelchair ramps and double slides. Neighborhood playgrounds or parks offer the opportunity to use large play equipment or have special programs.

Adaptive equipment had traditionally been used by those with special needs. But, for children with significant disabilities, conventional toys may not be appropriate. Recognizing the need for modified and original toys, a biomedical engineer has developed several and now heads his own organization. "Toys for Special Children."

The Boy and Girl Scouts of America provide scouting for the handicapped. Since its founding in 1910, the Boy Scouts of America has had participating members with physical or mental disabilities. Dr. James E. West, the first Chief Scout Executive, was handicapped, and as early as 1923, a special badge was created for those Scouts unable to pass certain requirements. Today Chapters are issued to community and national organizations to operate groups.

Many residential facilities provide summer camp and also reserve space for outside summer campers. Camp Keystone in Pennsylvania offers a specialized recreational program including ball fields, hiking trails, swimming and equipment for other activities. Campers sleep in heated cabins and enjoy the fun and games associated with a camp environment provided by a specially trained staff.

For children with multiple disabilities, the Institute of Logopedics in Kansas, has a Summer program for children from six to 22. Summer students participate in education and life-skill training in addition to camp and recreation.

Camp Huntington was established in 1961 as a residential summer camp for mild to developmentally disabled children in upstate New York. Some camps include siblings and parents in their programs. Various organizations may provide further information.

Camp can make a "special" Summer for special needs children. The American Camping Association has a national directory of camps that is cross referenced according to disabilities.

SPECIAL OLYMPICS

The concept of the Special Olympics began in the 1960's when Eunice Kennedy Shriver, President Kennedy's sister, started a day camp for people with mental retardation and realized they were far more capable in sports and physical activities than many experts believed. In 1968, she founded the Special Olympics and organized the first International

Games.

Prior to that time, there were no organized sports for special children. This international program of year-round sports training and competition has provided opportunities for over one million mentally retarded children and adults to participate in individual and team sports.

Programs take place in 25,000 communities in every state where athletes train and compete annually in local chapter and national games. The eighth annual Summer Special Olympic Games in Minneapolis, Minnesota, was the largest sporting event in the world in 1991.

"There is nothing in the world like Special Olympics," says Eunice Kennedy Shriver. "Nowhere else do we rejoice in how marvelous individuals with mental retardation are and celebrate the wonderful things they can achieve."

There is also the World Championships for Disabled Youth. More than 650 athletes from 20 countries competed in 1989 including 44 young athletes with disabilities from the United States.

On a smaller scale, parents sometimes organize their own sports leagues. That's what the parents of Timothy S. Cangialosi did in Fort Lauderdale, Florida. Called TSC for The Special Child, the program started in 1985 with five children. It grew in numbers, added a Miami chapter and another in Louisiana when a member moved there. Soccer is played from September to January and baseball from March to June. Local volunteer groups pick up the tab for uniforms and equipment.

"They're all winners," said Sharon Cangialosi. She explained there are no losers and that every season ends in a six-way tie for first place with each participant receiving a trophy.

Another sports milestone began in the Spring of 1990 when Little League baseball for the handicapped got underway for children from six to 18 years of age.

VACATION AND TRAVEL

Travel for those with special needs and their families takes extra planning and preparation to coordinate all the details. Some travel agencies have come to their aid and assist in travel plans by offering trips for individuals or specific groups and provide supervision for the travelers.

Parents who want to bring their handicapped children onto beaches and trails can use custom-built strollers. A wide variety of wheelchairs are available for the older child or adult. Playgrounds designed for the handicapped have therapeutic play units such as wheelchair swings.

The National Parks offer all Americans a wonderful outdoor experience. But, for millions of people who use a wheelchair or have a developmental disability, such enjoyment was limited.

To help them better enjoy the parks, over 60 health professionals and consulting editors who are themselves disabled, have put together a special guide-book which focuses on access in 37 different parks.

In addition to showing access for wheelchair users, there is information on everything from evaluation of restroom facilities to location of nearby hospitals. A series of single park guides will also be available.

Support organizations for various conditions can provide specific information. More programs and better equipment are making the lives of those with special needs better at home or away from home.

CHAPTER 7

ADOPTION –
AN ANSWER FOR SOME

Not all parents will bring their "special needs" baby home. Some will give their newborn up for adoption. For those who feel unable to cope with the complex situation, there is the adoption option.

More children with disabilities are being adopted today because fewer healthy babies are available. Childless couples were in the forefront of adoption for years. Although they are still in the picture, couples with birth children, older and single prospective parents have joined their ranks. Instead of the idealized baby, those with physical and/or mental handicaps are also being adopted. Clearly, the picture has changed.

Agencies that specialize in placing handicapped children often have more flexible requirements. Families who adopt come from all walks of life. The New York Spaulding for Children tells its applicants they look for parents for special children – families with room in their hearts and their homes. You can be single, married, divorced or widowed.

The Federal Government has taken steps to encourage

special needs adoption. Congress passed reforms of adoption and child welfare laws in 1980 offering a stipend for the first time to adoptive parents of special needs children. All states provide some adoption subsidies. Still, thousands of hard-to-place children are waiting to be adopted. Over 80 percent are older or special needs children. Recognizing the problem, President Bush announced legislative proposals in 1989 to encourage the adoption of children with disabilities. The bill allows a tax reduction of up to $3000 for expenses incurred in such adoptions.

Public agencies concentrate on special needs children but many private agencies are doing independent adoption in which birth parents place their child directly with adoptive parents. In many states independent placements are overtaking agency adoptions, although private adoption is prohibited in six states.

Massachusetts is a state where independent adoption is illegal. The Massachusetts Adoption Resource Exchange (MARE) provides service with chapters throughout the state and Project Impact works with the Department of Social Services to find families for children with special needs.

Each state has its own adoption laws as well as a public agency for care of children in the Division of Social Services. Agencies and adoption exchanges receive names of waiting children from both public and private agencies. Exchanges providing free services do not have children in their custody but take referrals and try to facilitate placement. Many agencies keep photo-listing books and descriptions of available children.

In traditional adoption the baby is separated from its "birth" parents legally and the adoptive parents take over with the child's past history sealed away. That veil of secrecy is being lifted in many cases as birth parents take an active role in the adoption process and even maintain some contact with the child and the adoptive parents. "Open" or cooperative adoption is the newer approach.

Changes in adoption have come about because of changes in attitude as well as a growing demand by adopted adults to know their roots. Advocates for open adoption say the risks are worth it and all parties can benefit.

"For most of our existence we followed traditional adoption procedures," explained Carol Rosik of Catholic Social Services of Wisconsin, a family and child welfare agency licensed by the state to place children in foster and adoptive care. "As we became more sensitive to requests from birth, foster and adoptive parents, we abandoned the casework approach and substituted open placement. We became convinced that these changes are an added healthy dimension to adoption, allowing more personal knowledge than documents can provide."

A poem, supporting open special needs adoption was written by adoptive parent Marcy Clausen in Adopting Children with Special Needs: A Sequel by Linda Dunn, Editor. (Published by North American Council on Adoptable Children, 1983.)

The following verses are from "Did You Think of Her Today?"

Oh, Woman, far away and gone
Birthmother of our child
I picture you and wonder
Did you think of her today?

Oh, Man not here, not known,
Whose spark of life knew no pain;
Who made this child, so dear to us
Did you think of her today?

Oh, Grandfather and Grandmother,
Caring, feeling, knowing what you've lost
Missing link in the family chain,

Lopped off limb from your tree,
Did you think of her today?

Years ago, as papers passed
from desk to desk,
Serving ties from you to her,
You hungered, wondered, ached to know,
A glimpse, a picture, anything
To ease the loss of that one child
You never were allowed to hold
Did you think of her today?

Other grandparents hold her now
But there was always room for you.
I often wish that you could know her
And share her growing years.
Your love is not a threat to ours
Could she ever have too much?
We have enough to share and open arms for yours,
But locked files and strangers' fears
Keep us far apart.

SPECIAL AGENCIES

In addition to state, regional and national exchanges, some agencies specialize in placing children with a specific disability, such as Down syndrome or spina bifida. The Spina Bifida Association of America has an Adoption Information Referral program that helps match infants and children with spina bifida to adoptive families.

More than 4000 American babies are born with Down Syndrome every year and some parents consider adoption. Janet Marchese, founder of the Down Syndrome Adoption Exchange, in White Plains, New York, helps many of them through this difficult time.

Started in 1976, the private, non-profit organization's primary purpose is to counsel parents and adoption agencies by providing information on support groups and other services. To date, D.S.A.E. has facilitated in the permanent adoption of over 1700 children with Down syndrome.

"We try to enlighten people about Down syndrome," says Janet, "because they can't make a decision without all the facts. We have to dispel some of the myths by getting people to see kids of all ages because a lot of professionals are not getting out and realizing what the potentials are."

"When we adopted our Down syndrome son 14 years ago," she explains, "we were told by a well educated social worker that he would be very low functioning and painted a very negative picture. I realized there were a lot of misconceptions from a lot of professional people, and unfortunately, it still happens today. People are not aware of what is available."

When parents consider relinquishing a child with Down syndrome, they can speak to other parents who tell them what it's like living with the disability.

Janet Marchese has turned to Charles and Emily Perl Kingsley many times to counsel new parents. As parents of a Down syndrome child, they let others know they're not alone.

"We've taken a lot of Janet's kids into our home right after they were born for a few days or weeks," says Charles. "It's a very difficult decision for many people. How do you make a life decision in three or four days?"

Emily has written a TV movie called "Kids Like These" and an article describing the experience of raising a child with a disability to try to help people understand and imagine how it would feel.

Susanna and Joseph Landa are parents who decided to give their baby up for adoption and were referred to Janet by the social worker at the hospital. They left their infant son in the

95

hospital, but when the final adoption papers hadn't been drawn up in two weeks, decided to take their baby home.

"I look back now," says Susanna, "and realize that I would have given up a baby that belongs to me and nobody else. It certainly would have been the wrong decision."

Amy White is another mother who almost gave up her child. She brought her baby home and spent a few weeks trying to care for him in a fog of depression. After reading about Janet, she called and asked for temporary foster care.

"I didn't know how long that was going to be, "says Amy. "I'd gotten names of birth parents, adoptive parents, people who had kept their children or given them up and called everybody I could. After speaking to all these people, going to programs, looking at different children of different ages, something in my heart told me we could be happy. I brought my baby home and he's the best thing that ever happened to me."

Another mother, Randy Wooldridge, decided on adoption. She took her baby home and was completely devastated. She saw Janet Marchese on TV and heard about an option she didn't realize existed.

"Janet gave me some suggestions and I talked to people like Amy White, who almost gave up her baby and then kept him," she said. "If we had to sign our baby to the social service network, we would have kept him and raised him and that would have been that. But, since we were able to choose the family, we made the decision to give him up for adoption."

Over 20 years ago, Dr. Michael Geraldi, a pediatrician, and his wife, Camille, a nurse, began taking care of infants and children with Down syndrome in Miami, Florida. Using their own finances and home, they have given loving care and medical attention to youngsters while providing therapy to the parents.

"We bridge the gap between keeping the baby and adoption", says Camille. "The need for this type of private environment is tremendous."

To provide for families nationwide, the Geraldi's formed the Up With Down Syndrome Foundation, which is dedicated to providing services that include counseling to the parents and families of these children as well as medical care and infant stimulation. Their dream, born out of necessity, is to expand present services, staff and housing facilities. The goal is to build a farm that will include a workshop, fruit grove and nursery with the entire enterprise operated by the handicapped.

"By early intervention, using infant stimulation and continued caring, we encourage the children towards independence or semi-independence," Camille said.

In addition to two natural daughters, the Geraldi's have adopted 17 children, 14 with Down syndrome and three with other handicaps.

Miami's Mayor, Stephen Clark, proclaimed December 4, 1988, as Camille and Dr. Michael Geraldi Day, in recognition of their outstanding contributions.

"We receive referrals from all over the country of newborns with Down syndrome," says Camille. "The hospital social work network comes together nationwide to make a very difficult time for new parents a little easier."

Camille counsels many new parents of Down syndrome babies. It doesn't always lead to adoption.

"My son was born in 1989," said one mother. "I knew prior to his birth that it would be a boy from ultrasound, but what I didn't know was that he would be born with Down syndrome. It was something my husband and I knew nothing about or were ever expecting to learn about."

"While I was in the hospital a nurse spoke to me about Camille and the work she does with these children. I got in touch with her and for the first time saw some light at the end of the tunnel where there was none."

"Camille and Michael Geraldi are two of the most special

people we have ever met," said another parent. "From the moment our son was born they have given us constant support, encouragement, knowledge and love. Camille met with us every week since his birth to teach us exercises and we watched our baby go from floppy to energetic in three months. We are totally and eternally thankful."

ROOM FOR ONE MORE

Many adoptive parents of special needs children always seem to have "room for one more." Ten or twelve special needs children doesn't seem so special to them.

Frank and Mary Torro have opened their home to ten physically and mentally handicapped children. They were married in 1969 and had two healthy children. Then in 1977 they had a daughter born with spina bifida and hydrocephalus. Her birth introduced them to the world of the severely handicapped. Social workers told them to institutionalize their daughter, but they took their baby home. Today, she is in junior high. One day they heard about a boy with spina bifida, hydrocephalus and cerebral palsy. His parents wouldn't take him home, so the Toros did. Now, he goes to school in a wheelchair. A needlepoint on the wall of their home says it all. "We'll Always Have Room for One More."

Amy and Gary Hutton of West Palm Beach, Florida, always seem to have room for more. They have adopted ten special needs children and have three "home grown" as they refer to their biological children.

"Our third adopted child was going to be the last one," Amy said. "He was our first Down syndrome baby and died from a heart defect."

"He was such a neat kid," said Gary. "It became a turning point and set us in the direction of adopting Down syndrome babies. We felt very comfortable with these children, and our youngest six all have Down syndrome.

"I love these kids," says Amy. "I think of parenting as a profession. There's a lot of networking involved and sometimes we deal directly with the birth parents because we're not threatened by them. Since more people are adopting Down syndrome babies today, we're thinking of taking cocaine babies. We'll take six more now."

For some adoptive parents, it began with foster care and when the opportunity to adopt came along, they went along. That's what happened to Kathie and Robert Migliaccio of Pennsylvania.

"We started with foster care and went on to adopt." said Kathie, who has seven biological children. "Then we just kept taking children that others didn't want."

In all, they have adopted 25 children. Their home has grown to keep pace and includes 17 bedrooms, classroom and therapy rooms. Their family car is a 40 foot bus that comes in handy when this family goes on vacation.

Kathie, who has appeared on the Phil Donahue show, has some words of advice for new parents of a special needs baby: "I would suggest trying private guardianship before adoption. It allows the parents a cooling down period. It's hard to make a decision in a few days. This way it can be temporary or permanent."

Adoption is an alternative for parents of a baby born with a disability. They don't usually have months of pregnancy to consider options. To help them make an informed decision, they can begin by contacting local agencies listed in the telephone book under Adoption or Social Services. Some provide counseling and the state agency answers questions about adoption in that particular state. The North American Council on Adoptable Children (NACAC) is an umbrella organization for adoptive parents and parent groups in the United States and Canada.

CHAPTER 8

BRAVE NEW WORLD

The hope is in the Future – that genetic science will advance far enough to offer new alternatives and possible cures for most birth defects. Researchers are getting closer to that day as they diligently work on a "gene" map, the biggest undertaking in the history of biology.

The Human Genome Project underway in the United States and other countries is expected to take about 15 years and is awesome in more ways than one. It will cost $3 billion to search among some 3 billion base pairs of genetic material.

Locating and sequencing genes is an enormous task since there are an estimated 100,000 genes on the 23 pairs of chromosomes in each cell. Every gene contains information directing the cell to make a specific part of the body. Mapping the genome (set of all genes) is a key to diagnosing and treating inherited disease.

The goal is to identify these mapped genes, decipher their coded messages and find out what they do. Thanks to sophisticated technology, more powerful computers are speeding up the work. Utilizing new techniques that open doors to the previously hidden world of molecular genetics, it is now possible to isolate genes.

"By mapping genes, you can find and isolate them and develop new means of therapy," said Yale geneticist Frank Ruddle. It is possible that the entire human genome will be mapped by the end of the 20th century.

Scientists knew chromosomes were largely made up of DNA (deoxyribonucleic acid) but in the 1950's the DNA structure was discovered, and in the late 1970's the process of gene-splicing was developed. The biotechnological revolution made possible the potential for treating certain genetic disorders, using high tech machines to find and decode genes.

After specific genes are located, researchers can begin to understand how the genes work and how they can be altered to treat or prevent the disease they cause.

It is only fitting that James Watson heads the government's enormous Genome Project, since he and Francis Crick opened the new genetic age in 1953 when they discovered DNA structure. It showed that the secret of life was knowable and all scientists had to do was develop tools to explore the new domain. By 1989, a new scanning microscope produced the first actual picture of a DNA molecule and it looked exactly like they said it would.

"We never foresaw anything like this," Watson says. "Now there is a revolution in what we can do. Some call it a Brave New World, but it's going to be a wonderful world for genetics."

GENETIC ENGINEERING

Genetic engineering is a way to fix faulty genes and will be part of a medical revolution in the 21st Century. The tools of genetic engineering are enabling scientists to trace defective genes, unravel their mystery and solve the problems they create.

The gene hunters predict they can find all the genes. Of the approximately 100,000 genes that make up a human being, nearly 5,000 have been identified and new ones are discovered every few days.

The new era of genetics is changing medicine by its focus on saving and improving the lives of those suffering from genetic diseases. The first major clinical institution, the $100 million Beckman Center for Molecular and Genetic Medicine, opened at Stanford University in 1989. Its goal is to translate molecular biology discoveries into new approaches to prevention and treatment of genetic diseases.

"We're committed to the basic thesis that the future of medicine is going to be at the level of understanding genes and molecules," said Nobel Prize winner Paul Berg, who heads the Stanford Center.

Johns Hopkins Medical Institutions opened a center for Medical Genetics in 1989 and a Gene Therapy Institute was established at the University of Michigan. A new Research Institute concentrating on molecular genetics and diseases that cause mental retardation opened in 1990 at Miami Children's Hospital in Miami, Florida.

As genes are found, genetic engineering techniques can be used to transplant them into animals that serve as models for human disease. They are also extracting genes from people and putting them into bacteria, which then become biochemical factories producing proteins never available before.

By having access to unlimited quantities of the body's natural substances, doctors are doing the previously impossible, such as using human growth hormone to eliminate dwarfism.

As early as 1983 scientists found the general location of the gene responsible for Huntington's disease, an inherited neurological disease.

In 1986, Harvard researchers led by Louis M. Kunkel,

103

pinpointed the problem gene in Duchenne muscular dystrophy, a crippling disease that strikes one in every 3,500 newborn males. By decoding the defective gene which is the blueprint for the dystrophin protein found in muscles, gene therapy is closer. Discovery of the gene and protein disorders underlying Duchenne muscular dystrophy had historic implications. The technology of "molecular genetics" successful in this research makes it possible to identify causes of the other genetic diseases.

The discovery that Down syndrome is linked to a defect on a tiny slice of one chromosome was an important step toward treating another of the most common genetic ailments. As scientists search for the precise gene responsible, they hope to develop a genetic therapy to eventually prevent it.

One of the most exciting discoveries in the history of genetic research came in 1989 when researchers located the defect in the gene that causes cystic fibrosis, the most common fatal birth defect in the United States.

Knowing what causes the diseases is the breakthrough scientists need to find a cure. New ways of treating birth defects can come from such basic understanding. Once a gene's code is known, it can be duplicated in the laboratory.

By finding the protein made by the defective cystic fibrosis gene, the door was opened to potential therapies that include an aerosol protein spray, the transfer of healthy genes or drugs designed to supply the missing protein.

Using genetic technology, a new purified human version of a drug compound is under development for cystic fibrosis. The product, called DNase, is designed to liquify the thick mucus associated with CF. In 1990, Genentech, a pharmaceutical company, applied to the Food and Drug Administration to begin testing this product.

The Cystic Fibrosis Foundation is cautiously optimistic about continued research into this product and supports the studies on its value for cystic fibrosis. The DNase work symbolizes the wide spectrum of approaches that the Foundation encourages to bring about new treatments for the children and young adults who have this disease today.

Another disease where there is hope for the first time is neurofibromatosis. The genetic research techniques already developed gave NF researchers a start and they closed in on chromosome 17 trying to find the exact defect. In July, 1990, they identified the culprit gene that causes the disease, the first step to a cure.

Recent discoveries are giving hope to all those suffering with genetic diseases that there might be a cure in time to help them. The hope is to create more effective therapies and to improve treatment for all the "special" children and that research will find the means to prevent handicaps so tomorrow's children may be spared today's problems.

"Our hope is genetics and our future is genetics," said Dr. Victor McKusick, a foremost genetic scientist, speaking at the 1989 National Conference of the United Leukodystrophy Foundation.

In a landmark project, human geneticists and veterinary researchers joined forces in 1990, using the new tools of genetic engineering to prevent hereditary diseases in dogs. About 40 percent of purebred canines are affected by genetic abnormalities.

"We are going to wipe out as many genetic diseases as we can," said Dr. George Brewer, professor of genetics at the University of Michigan, who is directing teams of scientists in a five-year project.

Using genetic analysis, they expect to hunt for and find the 400 defective dog genes and develop simple blood tests to identify the animals that carry them.

It was a particular disease in dogs that led Dr. Brewer to create the project. He is a specialist in the human equivalent, Wilson's disease.

"We're developing genetic markers for Wilson's disease," he

said. "I realized that's all we really need in dogs. While we can't do much about reproductive decisions in humans, we can control these matters in dogs." That's good news for the nation's 50 million dog-owning families.

GENE THERAPY

The first step in finding the cure for genetic diseases is to locate the problem gene. Once identified, "gene therapy" makes it possible to duplicate a healthy version. The ultimate correction strategy is to replace or correct the defective gene or add a normal one to provide the missing function.

Cystic fibrosis lends itself to a potential cure by replacing a defective gene with a normal one to override the undesirable effects and change cells from being carriers of disease.

"This revolutionary new area of medicine appears to be especially relevant to cystic fibrosis," said Dr. Robert J. Beall of the Cystic Fibrosis Foundation.

The March of Dimes launched a program to advance genetic therapy as a means of preventing birth defects and supported researchers who corrected a genetic defect that causes thalassemia in a test tube experiment and are hopeful this will lead to effective gene treatment.

A strain of mice has been created to advance the search for causes of disease. In a new gene switching method, a normal gene will replace an abnormal one in the mice.

Sickle cell anemia treatment is much closer since a research team genetically engineered a strain of mice to have the defective hemoglobin and hope to develop a way to insert a normal gene into blood-forming cells.

In clinical trials, hydroxyurea was a somewhat effective drug to treat this blood disorder. It activates a gene that functions in fetuses to regulate production of hemoglobin, the blood protein defective in those with sickle cell anemia. A search is on for drugs to do this better and more safely.

A new program in Molecular and Genetic Medicine at Stanford University is supporting research into the genetic basis for a variety of diseases. In addition to gene therapy, scientists are pursuing other approaches to correct genetic defects.

One medical program includes a genetics clinic to provide testing and information for people with inherited diseases. At the Marfan clinic, those with the disease get the expertise of a variety of specialists to treat the syndrome while geneticists and social workers provide counseling.

This combined effort approach is spreading. A Williams Syndrome Clinic was established in 1988 at Texas Children's Hospital in Houston, to conduct research with a team of specialists and in 1989, another WS Clinic opened at Children's Hospital Medical Center in Cincinnati, Ohio, to evaluate patients and provide information and counseling to families as well. In 1990, a new Williams Syndrome Clinic opened at the Children's Hospital in Boston to serve the unique medical, developmental and therapeutics needs of children with the syndrome and collect information that will be shared with other families.

One of the many strategies to overcome the problems of getting genes into cells that need them is with transplantable skin cells that can carry healing genes and may be useful against hemophilia and other disorders. The goal of cell therapy is to introduce normal cells that can combine with disease cells to provide the missing gene and its product.

On the cutting edge, a new treatment for Duchenne muscular dystrophy uses cell therapy to introduce normal cells called myoblasts. Researchers succeeded in myoblast transfer as a way to supply correct genetic information by injecting immature donor cells into a boy's foot muscle at the University of Tennessee. The healthy cells began making the missing protein that DMS patients lack.

"I think this is the opening salvo of what's going to happen in the 1990's, which I hope is going to be the successful treatment of many genetic disorders," said one of the doctors.

Other researchers have succeeded in injecting genes directly into muscles in experiments involving laboratory mice, setting the stage for use in humans.

The first attempt at human gene therapy won the unanimous backing of a National Institutes of Health panel in 1990, paving the way to treat children with a rare genetic disease by inserting new genes into their blood cells.

In 1991, scientists made a synthetic form of the gene linked to Duchenne muscular dystrophy, a giant step forward toward gene therapy for the disease.

NEW DRUG THERAPY

An unusual new form of drug treatment for the rare severe combined immunodeficiency disease (SCID), also known as Bubble Boy Disease, is the first of a new generation of drugs.

These children, born without a working immune system, had to live in sterile chambers because they can't resist infections. For 30 years, the recognized pattern of the disease led to death.

They are now being kept alive with supplements of proteins the defective genes don't make, all made possible because the defect was discovered.

"This is a milestone," said Dr. Michael Hershfield, a Duke University biochemical geneticist, who is treating some of these children with the new therapy.

In 1972, a doctor discovered that an enzyme called adenosine deaminase (ADA) was missing from the blood cells of two children with SCID. That discovery led investigators to try to understand the link between the missing enzyme and the immune system. Treatments included risky bone marrow transplants and red blood cell transfusions. By knowing that the absence of a single enzyme causes the disease, enzyme replacement was tried, but not very successfully since the enzymes were destroyed before they got to the cells that needed them.

In the 1970's, a process chemically linking a polymer (PEG) to an enzyme, offered hope. Biochemists at Enzon, Inc. found that by attaching this chemical process it allowed the enzyme to circulate in the bloodstream much longer than those untreated. It looked like this could be used for ADA deficiency.

Clinical trials began at Duke University in 1986 using the PEG modified enzyme. The first test was on a three year-old girl who failed to benefit from a bone marrow transplant.

"It was quite remarkable," Dr. Hershfield said. "It began to work immediately. She stayed at Duke for three months and then was able to go home and get the injections from her local physician."

Results were the same for the rest of the children treated and they are even going to school. For these children, the new genetics is already keeping its promise. Just a few years ago, they would not have been alive.

When the drug was approved by the FDA March 23, 1990, it was a milestone in medicine as the first effective form of enzyme replacement therapy for any inherited enzyme deficiency disease.

Treatment began at Duke on the 14th child in April, 1990, with proof that this new technique works and is safe. As the first of a new generation of drugs, it promises to transform the treatment of many genetic diseases.

The lifesaving modified enzyme was developed by Enzon, a small pharmaceutical company, under the Orphan Drug Act for "orphan diseases" that afflict under 200,000 people. The act offers tax incentives for clinical trial costs, but drug production costs are extremely high and the patient population extremely low. Small start-up companies are often the only ones willing to take orphan-drug risks. The next step to ensure treatment for this and other rare genetic disorders is to expand the existing law.

Not only are rare diseases affected by a money crunch, but even the most common ones are facing difficulties. The National Institutes of Health used to help the Cystic Fibrosis Foundation but in 1990, CFF had to give NIH $2 million dollars.

Identical twin boys were four years old when their parents were told they had a rare inherited disorder known as Batten's disease, that blinds, disables and always kills. After researching the disease, the parents made several trips to the NIH to find out more.

"I'm appalled there is so little being done and so little money available," the father of the victims said. "I find that it is a truly small group of dedicated people who are working for research funding."

It's obvious that continued research requires necessary funding and hopefully a way will be found to overcome those hurdles as well as the diseases.

Research! America, a non-profit organization led by former Senator Lowell Weicker, works to build public support and increase the budget for medical research.

Their message is clear: "The health of tomorrow's children and the hope of millions of Americans now living with incurable diseases depend on discoveries that come from today's biomedical research laboratories.

As researchers complete the Human Genome map, they will travel a new road leading to intervention, cure and prevention of genetic diseases.

CHAPTER 9

GENETIC COUNSELING
AND TESTING

In the last few decades, there has been an explosion of information in the field of human genetics, that branch of science dealing with heredity. Genetic counseling is a medical specialty that uses the latest information on birth defects and inherited diseases to assist families make informed personal decisions on pregnancy and the care of a child with a defect.

A genetic counselor translates genetic concepts into understandable and practical information, thereby helping families understand the mechanisms of inheritance. With nearly 4,000 identified birth defects, the total number of affected families is in the millions.

"We're here to help couples understand their options so they can make informed choices," said one counselor. "We're not here to tell them what to do."

Birth defects may be inherited, result from environmental factors or occur sporadically with no way to predict them in advance. Genetic counselors often estimate the probability that a certain abnormality will recur in the same family by evaluating results from laboratory tests, family history and basic laws of heredity.

Genetic services are available for couples who suspect their future children may be at risk of inheriting a disorder. There may be a history of a birth defect in the family or they may already have had a child with a disorder. If there is risk, a counselor will define the odds, discuss potential treatment or the likelihood of recurrence.

Before a family gets genetic counseling, the correct diagnosis of the birth defect is crucial. Many parents take their baby home and don't find out for months that there is a problem, and then longer to diagnose specifically.

After Bill and Nancy Dunklee took their baby home, they knew he was developmentally delayed, but didn't discover the cause until he was two. Their genetic specialist diagnosed Rubinstein-Taybi Syndrome and told them their baby could have been diagnosed at birth had anyone known what to look for.

Recent research has added greatly to the usefulness of genetic services by providing a variety of tests, including chromosome studies, tissue cultures, molecular and biochemical analysis for diagnosis and treatment as well as accurate information.

Diagnosis should be established by biochemical, genetic or chromosome study at a genetic center when a chromosomal disorder is suspected and the chromosomes of both parents studied to determine if the disorder is inherited. This is especially important if future pregnancies are planned.

A new generation of genetic counselors are trained at the master's level. This specialty didn't even exist twenty years ago, but genetic counseling is playing an increasing role by providing prenatal information to couples. Counselors not only explain genetics but play a postnatal role to help parents get new information about treatments for their child who has a birth defect.

There are more than 200 comprehensive genetic services centers in the United States that are usually located in obstetric or pediatric departments at large medical centers or teaching hospitals. Smaller localities far from such centers are served by satellite clinics.

PRENATAL TESTING

Today, medical science can diagnose some 250 birth defects in the unborn fetus by prenatal testing. Relatively simple tests have made it possible to predict certain defects before birth.

Ultrasound, the use of sound waves to show specific physical outlines, can detect or rule out a number of genetic disorders, such as fetal heart conditions, which can effectively be treated before birth.

Amniocentesis, usually performed between the 14th and 15th week of pregnancy, involves analyzing a small amount of amniotic fluid which can yield genetic information for analysis.

A newer diagnostic technique, chorionic villus sampling (CVS) can be performed earlier at eight to 11 weeks of pregnancy with chromosome analysis or other tests performed on cells from the placenta. New tests have opened the way for more noninvasive alternatives to current prenatal screening tests.

"One new test coming into use is the alpha-fetoprotein, or AFP-Plus, which calculates the risk in 65 percent of pregnancies affected by Down syndrome and certain other birth defects," said Dr. Barbara Burton, director of the Center for Medical and Reproductive Genetics at Michael Reese Hospital in Chicago, a newly created state-of-the-art center.

Prior to this test, the conventional screening method was for high-risk women aged 35 or over and detected only 20 percent of affected pregnancies. The new test (AFP) isn't really new because it was used for 15 years to screen neural tube defects such as spina bifida. About five years ago, an association was made between low levels of AFP and the occurrence of Down syndrome.

The advantage of this blood test is in being able to identify the unexpected high-risk patient, such as women under 35. Using a single sample of the pregnant woman's blood, AFP-Plus screens for both Down syndrome and open neural tube defects and may be offered to pregnant women between 15 and 20 weeks of pregnancy.

This test identifies those at risk who may then proceed to more definitive diagnostic testing such as ultrasound and amniocentesis. Many obstetricians now routinely offer their pregnant patients the option of taking the blood test. In California, the law requires doctors to offer every pregnant woman the AFP blood test.

Ultrasound scans can accurately check a fetus for spinal abnormalities and some other birth defects. Women with an elevated AFP level and a normal ultrasound could use this in place of amnio, which carries a 1 in 500 risk of miscarriage. Ultrasound poses no known risk to the fetus.

With prenatal screening, parents whose offspring are at risk for an inherited disease face the choice of therapeutic abortion or giving birth to a child with the defect. In some cases, parents know the child with a specific disease will suffer and die.

The decision about testing for fetal chromosomal abnormalities is a very personal one that should be made early in the pregnancy. Any questions regarding available tests may be directed to one's doctor or a trained genetic counselor.

New tests are opening the way for more alternatives to current prenatal screening tests. Cordocentesis or percutaneous umbilical blood sampling (PUBS) and fetal blood sampling (1986) are relatively new procedures that test the fetus for chromosome abnormalities.

Since some fetus cells leak into the mother's bloodstream after the eighth week of pregnancy, National Institute of Child Health and Human Development researchers are working to develop procedures to separate fetal cells from maternal circulation for use in prenatal diagnosis of genetic disorders.

A Harvard medical team isolated fetal blood cells in blood taken from pregnant women in 1990. It is hoped these cells can be used to perform testing now being done by amnio or CVS. In 1991, researchers used new techniques to sift fetal blood cells to test for chromosome disorders.

Gene amplification detected chromosomal damage from a single fetal cell in a sample of the mother's blood in England. This departure from conventional screening methods could help doctors find defects without putting either the woman or fetus at risk.

Researchers are on the cutting edge of preconception genetic testing as an alternative to the decision of whether to abort or carry to term a fetus with a known defect. Doctors at the Reproductive Genetics Institute at Chicago's Illinois Masonic Medical Center are able to screen human eggs for abnormalities *before* pregnancy.

They use in vitro fertilization, a process in which egg and sperm are united outside the woman's body and then transferred into the woman's uterus. Doctors have gone from infertility therapy to genetic diagnosis.

"This procedure is for couples who already know they are carriers of a genetic disorder," explained Dr. Charles Strom, chief of medical genetics at one of the few pre-conception clinics in the United States.

Genetic analysis normally is performed after conception and pregnancy. In this pre-conception technique, mature eggs are removed and only healthy ones reinserted after fertilization.

"We worked with a couple who already have a child with cystic fibrosis and know they are at risk," said Dr. Strom.

The new technique of testing the woman's egg before it is

115

fertilized and discarding a defective one before conception is being used to detect muscular dystrophy, Tay-Sachs disease, hemophilia, sickle-cell anemia and other diseases.

Test-tube baby specialists recently established an egg donor program and reported their first pregnancy. In this case, the mother received eggs from a non-blood relative that were fertilized in the test tube by her husband. Because of genetic problems in her own eggs, there was a high risk of another child with severe defects. She had already given birth to two mentally retarded sons. The egg donor program is for couples who previously had children with genetic disorders attributed to the mother's egg.

In another study, eggs were collected from a woman and fertilized in a test tube, letting them grow three days before checking genetic material to indicate the presence of a Y chromosome (male). Since about 200 genetic diseases affect only boys, the findings were aimed at implanting a female embryo in cases where a boy could inherit a serious or fatal disease.

Tests are already available for a number of potentially damaging hereditary diseases. Some birth defects don't show up immediately. For some inherited disorders, simple blood tests identify carriers of serious blood disorders such as thalassemia, hemophilia and sickle cell anemia. It is recommended that all black Americans of child bearing age take the test for sickle cell anemia since it is found predominantly in the black population.

In 1971, by measuring a small amount of blood, an effective carrier test was developed for Tay-Sachs disease, in which a single enzyme is defective. Since nearly one out of 25 American Jews carries the Tay-Sachs gene, descendants of central and Eastern European Jews are primarily affected and pre-marital testing is suggested.

Before carrier testing, the only way to learn about the risk was after having a Tay-Sachs baby. Now, couples can know if they are at risk before such tragedy strikes. National Tay-Sachs and Allied Diseases Association promotes genetic screening programs nationally through affiliated hospitals and regional chapters.

"When my first baby was born in the 1960's," one mother told me, "she was so beautiful and everything seemed perfect. By the time she was six months old, we knew there was something wrong. That's when symptoms of Tay-Sachs first appear and then progressively worsens with death by the age of three."

Because of premarital testing and carrier identification along with prenatal testing, this deadly and tragic disease has practically disappeared. Today, it is a genetic success story.

After prenatal tests became available for thalassemia in a British program, the number of children born with this inherited disorder fell by 78 percent. Prenatal diagnosis is also available for other genetic diseases including Duchenne muscular dystrophy, sickle cell anemia and Huntington's disease.

A new blood test developed for Batten's disease can pick up carriers by screening families with a history of the disease. Genetic counseling, especially premarital screening, could reduce the number of affected children. With a reliable blood test, genetic analysis will pinpoint the location of the gene involved which would help establish the basic cause of the disease.

Researchers found an enzyme deficiency linked to degeneration of the brain in Canavan disease. This discovery led to the development of a prenatal diagnostic test.

A simple new blood test may identify those at risk for developing diabetes, especially in families where one child already has it. Development of the test followed discovery of the genetic marker for diabetes. The hope is that the test used with preventive drugs under investigation will prevent the onset of the disease in the future.

117

After having a child with spina bifida, the risk increases in future pregnancies from one in 1000 to one in 40. Testing can detect spina bifida.

Discovery of genes that cause disease opens the way to better screening tests to determine which couples are at risk. These tests usually follow quickly.

In Huntington's disease, the symptoms don't appear until middle age and is unknowingly passed on as a dominant gene. One young woman with a PhD in psychology, whose mother had the disease, became a key player in the drama to find the elusive gene. She found herself in Venezuela in 1979 to study a family tree with thousands of descendants. She was searching for someone who had received two copies of the HD gene, one from each parent. She took blood samples of them and their children along with others there for testing by researchers in the United States.

As a result, Nancy Wexler and her colleagues announced they had found the genetic defect for Huntington's disease in 1983. This led to development of a screening test. Blood samples for genetic studies provide clues to solving the mystery of many disorders.

One of the most spectacular breakthroughs of the last decade was identification in 1989 of the gene that causes cystic fibrosis. Discovery of the gene on Chromosome 7, opened the way for screening tests.

About one in 25 Americans of European ancestry is a carrier of the cystic fibrosis gene, but there was no way to screen the general population. Carrier testing was only possible in families where the disease had already occurred.

The most immediate impact of the research is improved tests to screen for the disease. In the major mutation, or 70 percent of the chromosomes with the CF gene, there is a deletion of three bases that cause the gene to create a defective protein in the cell.

"In theory, we can do testing on these families," says Lap-

Chee Tsui, who discovered the errant gene. "Once the rest of the mutations are known, routine screening will be available." After the gene was discovered, a new test revealed over 75 percent of adults who risk having children with CF. As researchers close in on the remaining mutations, screening tests will be able to identify over 95 percent of the eight million American carriers.

The world's first population-wide screening program for CF got underway in London in 1990. Doctors conducting this pilot study offered the test to a target population of 200,000 people for two years.

"Discovery of the neurofibromatosis gene means testing will be available," said Dr. Mislen Bauer, Clinical Genetics Director of the NF Center at Miami Children's Hospital. "Until now, there was no way for prenatal diagnosis, either by genetic testing or ultrasonography. We expect such testing in the near future. Parents will know if their child has the disorder before spots or tumors appear."

Genetic testing will allow a precise diagnosis in those known to be at risk as well as prenatal testing to determine if the fetus has the NF gene. Because the gene is dominant, there is a 50 percent chance it may be passed on although half of all cases are spontaneous mutations. Severity of this disorder varies widely and its course is unpredictable.

"We must include explanations, education and counseling in a screening program," advises Dr. Francis Collins, who codiscovered the neurofibromatosis and cystic fibrosis genes. "It is important to know what it means if a person is a carrier so they can understand its implications."

The age of specialization has reached genetic counseling. At major medical centers, a medical genetics program was developed to provide testing and information on inherited diseases. Separate clinics for people with certain genetic diseases provide counseling from geneticists along with the expertise of other specialists.

The Genetic Services Center at Gallaudet Research Institute was established to study more than 200 known genetic forms of hearing impairment. Its primary function is to perform genetic evaluations and counseling sessions.

At the Neurofibromatosis Centers, a multi-disciplinary teamwork approach is used to provide comprehensive evaluations and referral services that include medical care and genetic counseling.

NEW ERA OF PRENATAL SCREENING

As more genes that cause congenital diseases are identified, a new era of prenatal screening has begun. DNA testing is already available at many major medical centers with the latest technology. This will allow screening of a fetus for a wider range of genetic diseases. Demand for testing has increased along with knowledge about birth defects.

DNA can be extracted from a fetal cell and a disease gene used as a probe that will seek its own likeness. If the probe finds a match, the fetus has the disease.

DNA testing can work even when a specific gene hasn't been identified. By using markers which are situated very close to the defective gene, it is possible to predict with up to 95 percent accuracy that the culprit gene is also there.

Presymptomatic testing is a new frontier that will provide counselors with new tests to determine whether an apparently healthy adult carries the genetic marker for such diseases as Huntington's which shows up later in life. These tests can also be performed on the fetus.

BEYOND PRENATAL TESTING

Even newborns undergo several screening tests today to detect possible birth defects before leaving the hospital.

Inborn errors of metabolism are examples of defects that are not immediately visible, but can cause mental retardation unless detected early.

The first newborn screening test made available was for phenylketonuria (PKU) which can result in mental retardation unless the baby is fed a special formula. In 1961, a March of Dimes researcher developed a simple test using a single drop of blood from the newborn's heel. Most states require screening for PKU and one or two other conditions. Some states have a law that requires newborns to be tested for sickle cell disease. In a number of states, all babies are tested at birth for two birth defects that can lead to mental retardation, PKU and congenital hypothyroidism (CH).

By the mid 1990's, geneticists predict new technology will make it possible to check newborns for as many as 15 inherited disorders. Newborns will have DNA information so those at risk can be identified and new therapies used to prevent or treat a condition.

An exciting area of study now centers on fetal diagnosis and treatment for the unborn. As development of more sophisticated diagnostic and detection procedures emerge, genetic counseling will play an even greater role tomorrow.

Anyone who thinks they would benefit from genetic counseling should call the nearest hospital associated with a medical school, ask a physician or contact a local chapter of the March of Dimes. If a specific disorder is suspected, contact that organization, The Alliance of Genetic Support Groups or the National Society of Genetic Counselors.

121

CHAPTER 10

THE FUTURE IS NOW

"The Doctor of the future will interest his patients in the cause and prevention of disease." Those words were spoken by Thomas Edison in the last century.

"We're looking at a totally new form of medicine," geneticist Michael Hayden said in 1990. "With preventive medicine, we'll be able to predict the risk of a disease and hopefully prevent its onset."

Important research advances have already started the 1990's on a path to a golden age of genetics. As researchers are mapping the human genome, health officials are mapping a strategy to improve the health of Americans by the year 2000.

"We can no longer ignore the fact that individually, and as a nation, prevention is the single most important factor in maintaining good health," said Dr. Louis Sullivan, Secretary of Health and Human Services.

By the 21st century, preventive medicine will enable doctors to predict and prevent many hereditary diseases as well as those without genetic origin.

PREVENTION

According to March of Dimes statistics, a number of birth defects are preventable. Reductions will come about by new information emerging on environmental factors including maternal infections, chemical exposure, radiation, pesticides, drugs and alcohol. Scientists all over the world are studying the increasing role that environmental agents play in causing birth defects.

Unnecessary drug prescriptions during pregnancy can cause defects and learning disabilities. Until birth defects appeared from use of the drug, thalidomide, in the early 1960's, obstetricians believed the fetus was protected from potentially harmful substances by the placenta.

In all, about 5,000 children were born disabled because of the drug. An American doctor, Frances Kelsey, of the FDA, kept thalidomide off the shelves in this country and set a precedent to protect the public from hasty drug testing.

The West German firm that manufactured the drug was sued for negligence, resulting in a fund to provide for the needs of affected children. The concept of corporate and government liability as to the safety of pharmaceutical products was born.

Betty Mekdeci founded the Association of Birth Defect Children (ABDC) in 1982 as a clearinghouse for information about environmental causes of birth defects as a result of her experience.

Her research helped link a commonly used drug to her son's birth defects. Although it was removed from the market in 1983, she realized the larger problem of birth defects caused by toxic environmental exposure during pregnancy.

Another drug, DES, used by pregnant women to prevent miscarriage was taken off the market after it was linked to a rare cancer and birth defects. Accutane, an acne drug, now carries a warning label for pregnant women, as do cigarettes and alcohol.

The Surgeon General's warning appears on cigarettes; "Smoking by Pregnant Women may result in fetal injury, premature birth and low birth rate." There is also a warning on alcoholic beverages.

"Many birth defects can be prevented by educating women of childbearing age about the dangers of drugs to unborn babies," says March of Dimes former National Board of Trustees chairman, John Henry Felix.

A combination of birth defects called fetal alcohol syndrome is caused by drinking heavily while pregnant. Cocaine is the most dangerous drug to unborn babies, some of whom are damaged while still in the womb and carry disabilities with them after birth.

Since evidence shows that drugs, chemicals and alcohol pass from the mother's bloodstream to the baby, pregnant women are advised to avoid them.

Over the past few years, there has been an increase in the number of pregnant women who use cocaine, and an alarming increase in the number of babies born affected (by the drug). The birth defects and other problems caused by cocaine use are entirely preventable.

Over the counter drugs are seen as potential toxins and some prescriptions like tranquilizers and barbiturates may increase the risk of birth defects. Experts recommend pregnant women check with their obstetrician before taking any drugs.

Other substances and exposure to radiation may also cause mental retardation or physical deformities. While only about five percent of birth defects can be directly attributed to toxic agents at the present time, increased research is aimed at identifying potentially hazardous substances and testing their effects.

The National Network to Prevent Birth Defects reports

progress in this area, especially regarding toxins. In California, certain businesses are required to warn of exposure to toxins that cause birth defects or cancer and forbids adding them to drinking water. The California Birth Defect Prevention Act forbids the sale of pesticides that cause birth defects or have not been tested. Stronger measures to limit the use of pesticides are being urged.

DDT was hailed as the world's most effective pesticide and was used for many years before there was any understanding of damage to the environment. It demonstrates the time gap between use and results.

The government acknowledged in 1990 that exposure to Agent Orange, the defoliant used during the Vietnam War, may have caused health problems to military personnel. It was hailed as a breakthrough in a decade-long argument over whether it caused a variety of birth defects and other conditions. That same year, medical records were released detailing the impact of low radiation on workers at government nuclear facilities dating back to the 1940's.

When too many cases of Down syndrome and other birth defects were found in a Texas town in 1990, 500 residents brought suit against a chemical plant they believed responsible for polluting air and water with toxins.

New awareness of hazards from toxic agents with the potential to damage a fetus are being studied to determine which substances may cause mental retardation or physical deformities. It is a worldwide problem and scientists are exploring how genes enact with the environment.

High levels of lead are known to cause mental retardation in infants of exposed mothers. Government regulation of lead has helped drop levels, due largely to lead-free gasoline, although exposure to lead is still very real from lead-based paint, contaminated soil or polluted water. The Department of Housing and Urban Development pushed for removal of lead paint in public housing.

Alarming levels of lead in Mexico City's air and water threatened a whole generation of pregnant women and their offspring, according to a three-year study released in 1990. Low birth weight and impaired mental development are great risks to children of women exposed to air polluted by exhausts from three million vehicles. Federal officials recognized dangerous air pollution levels and introduced oxygenated gasoline. Beginning in 1991, every car manufactured in Mexico is required to be equipped with a catalytic converter designed to cut polluting exhaust.

A Norwegian study estimated that nine percent of all birth defects stem from parental exposure to hazards in the workplace. Women in certain jobs are exposed to chemicals or radiation that may cause birth defects.

According to Reproductive Toxicology Journal, "Exposure of men to lead levels still considered acceptable in the industry may be associated with reproduction-related harm. Sources of danger to the fetus go beyond the workplace and cross the sex line, affecting men and women alike".

As computer use mushrooms, the number of video display terminals increases accordingly. It is known that VDT's emit several types of radiation and investigation is underway to determine possible reproductive problems associated with its use.

Of some 60,000 chemicals in wide commercial use, only three are officially regulated because of reproductive dangers. DBCP has been banned, while ethylene oxide, commonly used to sterilize surgical instruments, and lead have exposure limits and conditions for use.

Fewer toxic chemicals are in our air and water as the result of a 1990 revision of the Clean Air Act of 1970, the nation's main environmental protection. Reductions in the incidence of certain birth defects are the result of new anti-pollution measures.

Mounting evidence suggests that exposure to certain

127

environmental toxins may trigger onset of a particular disorder. Researchers are optimistic about identifying those at risk before it strikes.

It was concluded years ago that fetal exposure to radiation can lead to mental retardation. The National Research Council cautions pregnant women to avoid X-rays whenever possible, especially in the pelvic area, since there is already unavoidable radiation from natural sources such as cosmic rays and radioactive elements in the soil.

Radiation experts warn that women should be particularly cautious during the eight to 15 weeks after conception, when radiation exposure carries a risk of mental retardation in unborn children. This includes inflight radiation for pregnant women who are advised to limit flying time during pregnancy.

"It poses a risk," acknowledges a 25-year-old flight attendant who admits she is concerned. The Federal Aviation Agency issued a landmark advisory in 1990 telling crew members that flying high-altitude routes increased the risk of unsafe radiation to an unborn child.

Scientists are afraid the proportion of carriers of deleterious genes may be increasing by exposure to X-rays, fallout from radiation and even new migration and marriage patterns.

A molecular change affecting a gene is a mutation that is usually recessive and has no harmful effect unless the other gene in the pair has the same characteristics.

With every increase in carriers of a particular defective gene, there is a greater increase in the likelihood of a mating. Some genetic disorders are found to a greater extent among certain ethnic groups. Knowing one's family tree can be a guide to prevention and a vital aspect of family planning. Greater molecular understanding may lead to preventive measures that include certain vitamins to protect genes against mutations.

Viruses and other illness also have serious consequences for pregnant women. Over 20,000 babies were born with birth defects during a rubella (German measles) outbreak in 1964. Their mothers caught the disease while pregnant and unknowingly passed it on to their babies. Vaccination against rubella became possible in 1969, and although big outbreaks have been eliminated, it still occurs. The March of Dimes Foundation continues to educate about the need for vaccination.

Rubella is not the same as regular measles, called rubeola, and in 1989, 47 states and the District of Columbia had outbreaks. Anyone born after 1956 should be immunized and gamma globulin is recommended for pregnant women who have been exposed. Chicken pox during pregnancy can cause birth defects and pregnant women should contact their doctors if they have been exposed.

A major key to prevention is early identification of high risk fetuses and newborns so appropriate intervention or intensive service can be initiated promptly.

Neonatology, the care of premature or sick newborn babies, became a pediatric subspecialty in the last 25 years. Due to advanced technology, premature infants are not only surviving in greater numbers, but also with a greatly improved outcome.

In 1990, another new subspecialty was formally proposed to better address the needs of developmental pediatrics. It is for neurodevelopmental disabilities which include mental retardation and other disturbances of the nervous system, such as cerebral palsy. Dr. Ada Hayes of Philadelphia is one of this new breed of pediatricians and focuses on children with Down syndrome and mental retardation.

Premature birth is a leading cause of problems and efforts are being made to target teenagers and others at risk about getting better prenatal care.

Respiratory distress affects about 20 percent of the 250,000 premature babies born every year. Their immature lungs lack the chemical, surfactant, vital to proper breathing. An experimental drug, called Exosurf, appears to improve this condition and was approved by the FDA for use in hospitals with neonatal intensive care units.

Bleeding in the brain happens in about 40 percent of babies born at least 10 weeks early and can result in cerebral palsy and mental retardation. Doctors believe this occurs because the baby's blood vessels are too immature to stand the surges in blood pressure that follow delivery.

Dr. Walter J. Morales, director of maternal/fetal medicine at Arnold Palmer Hospital for Women and Children in Orlando, Florida, tried Vitamin K on 92 pregnant women expected to deliver prematurely because it aids in blood clotting in infants. Results were so encouraging that Dr. Morales now uses the Vitamin K treatment in any such pregnancy at risk.

A recent study found that women who take multivitamins with folic acid around the time of conception and during the first six weeks of pregnancy reduce the risk of certain birth defects by more than 50 percent. Neural tube defects such as spina bifida or anencephaly occur early in the pregnancy.

"This is a very important finding," said Dr. Donald Patrick, advisor to the Spina Bifida Association. "It is the first possible breakthrough in cause research in the last 20 years."

Intensive treatment before conception can greatly reduce the chances of diabetic women bearing children with birth defects. Heart and spinal abnormalities may occur in women with the highest levels of sugar in their blood.

Progress has been made in preventing cerebral palsy due to birth injury and in other cases, brain damage is minimized by early intervention. Improved prenatal care and prevention of the rh disease have cut the toll as well as early intervention. It is only the tip of the iceberg in discovering ways to treat and cure birth defects.

News was made in 1990 by dramatic surgery to correct a fetal diaphragmatic hernia, a severe defect that occurs in approximately one in 2,000 births every year. For the first time doctors performed successful major surgery on a fetus by

moving misplaced internal organs from the chest and correct-
ing the defect that kills three quarters of its victims before or
at birth. The operation was the most ambitious in the new
field of fetal surgery.   Minor bladder surgery had been
performed before but this was a milestone.

"What makes this so exciting is the promise it holds for the
future," said Dr. Richard Berkowitz of Mt. Sinai Medical
Center in New York.

Treatment before birth includes medication to reverse fetal
heart arrhythmias, transfusions for severe RH blood diseases,
hormones or vitamins to correct metabolic problems and
surgery to stop progressive damage caused by anatomical
malformations. Doctors think spina bifida may someday be
prevented by surgically patching the fetal spine before birth.

Gene therapy during pregnancy is a goal for the 21st
century and recent developments encourage scientists to
search for better ways to treat and cure birth defects.

RESEARCH ADVANCES

Research advances in the battle to conquer birth defects are
the legacy of the last decade of the 20th century.

Progress includes effective therapies and vastly improved
treatment. Perhaps the single most important result is that
after years of research, one advance leads to others.

"The discovery of the cystic fibrosis gene prepared the way
for other discoveries," said Dr. Aser Rothstein, Director of
Research Institute at The Hospital for Sick Children in
Toronto. Cystic fibrosis was still a mystery in 1980 with not
even a clue about where the problem gene was. By 1989,
researchers found it and the flaw that causes the fatal disease.

For children suffering with this genetic disorder, identification of the gene means there is a good chance for an effective
treatment or cure in their lifetime. It means they may not

131

have to die by the age of 30. It means there will be a test to determine the risk of having a child with cystic fibrosis.

"We hope to have an easy effective treatment, reduce symptoms and hopefully, not have such a horrible outcome," said Lap Chee Tsui of the Hospital for Sick Children in Toronto, who with Dr. Francis Collins of the University of Michigan, discovered the gene.

"Cystic fibrosis is very rare in China and there is no word for it because it occurs predominantly in Caucasians," said Tsui, a molecular biologist from Hong Kong.

"I had to look it up when I read about an opening for a CF researcher in Toronto. But, I wanted to apply my knowledge and training to discover the gene."

The search for the CF gene was competitive, but in the end, it was collaborative effort by Tsui and Collins. Their collaboration began in 1987, when the two who had been working independently, got together at a scientific meeting and continued to meet every few months. At the same time, Tsui was working with John Riordan, a membrane chemist and colleague. With clues from Riordan's libraries of genetic material, Tsui determined in March, 1989, they had found the gene. By May, they isolated the defect in the gene and made the announcement in August. Tsui says cooperation was necessary because of the amount of genetic ground to cover.

Dr. Francis Collins, who found the CF gene with Tsui, led one of the teams that discovered the gene for neurofibromatosis a year later. By using genetic research techniques already developed, a similar approach was used to pinpoint the NF gene.

This process opens the door wider for scientists to close in on other genetic diseases. A month after finding the gene responsible for the disfiguring and potentially deadly NF disease, researchers discovered how the gene may cause it. This disorder was known for over 100 years but only after isolation of the gene is improved treatment possible.

There are strong indications that the protein responsible for NF is related to proteins involved in certain cancers. It is an example of how the door opens to develop new treatments for a specific disorder, but can also lead to new treatments for others.

In the decisive decade of the 1990's researchers found new clues to the cause of the Marfan Syndrome, a baffling hereditary disease best known for its role in the sudden deaths of famous athletes such as Olympic volleyball star Flo Hyman.

Scientists identified the gene responsible for the inherited disorder in July, 1991. This discovery could lead to better treatments. The hope is to identify infants with the disease, predict who will have serious complications and use strategies to control or correct it.

The gene that causes fragile X syndrome, the most common form of mental retardation, was discovered in 1991 and researchers have developed a laboratory test to help identify babies.

WHAT DISCOVERY OF THE NEUROFIBROMA-TOSIS GENE MEANS TO:

A 47-year old mother who knew she had NF. What she didn't know was that because it is a dormant gene, she could pass the disorder on to her child.

"No one ever told me it was hereditary," said Fran Kartz, whose 19-year-old son also has NF. "Discovery of the gene is great news. I hope there's a cure soon, if not for me, then for my son."

A molecular biologist who knows the intricacies of genetics. As the mother of a beautiful nine-year-old daughter, she knows first hand about genetic diseases. Her daughter, who has NF as the result of a spontaneous mutation, has seen some people with the tumors and asks if she's going to look like that.

"We're just waiting, waiting to wait, knowing it never ends," said the mother who dedicated her thesis to her daughter. "Maybe research will arrest the progress of the disease or provide better treatment."

A young mother never heard of NF before her son was diagnosed when he was less than a year old.

"I was hysterical when I found out," she said. "I realized that anyone can get anything at any time with a new mutation."

"My son is three and doesn't have any other signs beside the tell-tale coffee-colored spots. I'm hopeful they will have a drug or something in a few years."

A young father didn't have any obvious symptoms of NF, although his brother did. Now his baby daughter was diagnosed with it before her first birthday and he learned the hard way that he is a carrier.

Another father with NF only had spots and didn't know it was hereditary. Now his 13 year-old daughter also has spots and is at the age where she is self conscious.

"There is no way to tell how severe progression will be," he said. "I just hope she will benefit from recent advances."

A 71-year-old woman who found out what her spots meant when she was over 40. She married late in life and had no children so she never had to deal with that problem.

"Adults need help emotionally," she says. "Especially when you get these ugly tumors all over your face. I got involved with the NF Center in my area and its been a big help."

A doctor who is medical director of two NF Centers in South Florida, sees a light at the end of the tunnel.

"Before there was nothing, now there is hope," said Dr. Mislen Bauer.

GENETICS ARE HERE NOW

A revolutionary "first" human gene therapy treatment was performed September 14, 1990, on a four-year-old girl suffering from an immune deficiency defect.

This historic procedure paved the way for inserting disease-curing genes into human cells of those suffering from other serious disorders. It may hold the key for treating many birth defects sooner than anyone dreamed of.

One week later researchers announced another milestone. They corrected the biochemical defect that causes cystic fibrosis by inserting a healthy gene into diseased cells grown in a test tube.

Working independently, two groups corrected the cell defect that causes the lungs to produce thick mucus setting the stage for fatal lung infections.

"By giving cells a normal copy of the cystic fibrosis gene, the chloride ions that cannot be expelled in CF patients began to behave normally," said Dr. Michael Welsh of the University of Iowa College of Medicine in Iowa City, co-author of a report published in the British journal *Nature*. "The normal gene corrected the defect by directing cells to produce a particular protein."

The CF gene encodes a membrane protein that researchers studied. Understanding the genetic basis provides the foundation for developing treatments. It is another milestone en route from genetic defect to effective therapy.

"We're talking a few years in terms of a cure," said Robert Beall, medical director of the Cystic Fibrosis Foundation.

"We're very excited because it gives us tremendous hope that gene therapy is going to become a reality for cystic fibrosis patients."

It brings the day closer when disease-curing genes are used for hemophilia, sickle cell anemia, Huntington's disease,

135

neurofibromatosis, muscular dystrophy and countless other disabling conditions. Advances in genetic therapy will bring about dramatic changes in the pharmaceutical industry as well.

As is often the case of biomedical research, progress in one area leads to another. As little as ten years ago, researchers were still in the dark about most genetic diseases and the possibility of curing them. The light has turned on with astonishing brightness in a short time and offers great hope for the next ten years and a still brighter tomorrow.

By the 21st century, many children will be spared the problems of today as medical science will be able to cure a variety of diseases. The hope of the future is to eliminate many birth defects in future generations.

We have come to expect the unexpected. Someday, we may not have to expect "the unexpected child."

RESOURCE LIST

This resource section is a reference for parents and professionals who live and work with Special Needs Children. From the time a child is born or recognized with a disability, parents need information about the condition, available services and where to locate those services.

It is important for parents to utilize the resources available in order to accentuate the "abilities instead of the disabilities" of their child.

The list includes national and local organizations that provide information on a variety of issues. Each chapter has a directory of specific groups that can answer questions covered in that chapter, although they may overlap from time to time.

An example is The National Information Center for Children and Youth with Handicaps. Since 1982, they have been collecting and sharing information helpful to families with a disability. The Center answers questions, links people to experts in special education, therapies, parent training and much more. It serves as an exchange network keeping track of all organizations concerned with disability issues.

"Like so many other mothers, I learned about disability issues, programs, services, support groups, medical services,

insurance and education through the school of hard knocks,"
said Susan Ripley, Deputy Director and Information Services
Manager for NICHCY." After years of searching, I found
some answers, but the help I needed was there all the time,
if only I had known who to call."

Many organizations have toll free numbers and will put you
in touch with local groups for easier access to resources.
There is a wonderful world of networking to help you.

CHAPTER ONE: YOUR SPECIAL BABY

The Federal Government operates a number of clearinghouses and information centers that provide referrals and publications.

Department of Health and Human Services, National Institutes of Health
Bethesda, Maryland 20892
(800) 638-6833

Health Hotlines lists organizations with toll-free numbers for information and services. Contact: Specialized Information Services National Library of Medicine
8600 Rockville Pike
Bethesda, MD 20894

National Health Information Center lists toll-free numbers for information and publications.
NHIC
P.O. Box 1133
Washington, DC 20013-1133
(800) 336-4797

National Information System and Clearinghouse provides information on services for children in every state
(800) 922-9234

National Information Center for Children and Youth With Handicaps
P.O. Box 1492
Washington, DC 20013
(800) 999-5599

Clearinghouse on Handicapped and Gifted Children
Council for Exceptional Children
1920 Association Drive
Reston, VA 22091

National Center for Education in Maternal and Child Health
38th and R Streets NW
Washington, DC 20057
(202) 625-8400

National Birth Defects Center
30 Warren Street
Brighton, MA 02135
(617) 787-5958

Heredity Disease Foundation
1427 Seventh Street
Santa Monica, CA 90401
(213) 458-4183

National Easter Seal Society
70 E. Lake Street
Chicago, IL 60601
(313) 667-7400

National headquarters for the **March of Dimes Birth Defects Foundation** is 1275 Mamaroneck Avenue, White Plains, New York 10605 (914) 428-7100.

National Rehabilitation Information Center (NARIC)
8455 Colesville Road
Suite 935
Silver Spring, Maryland 20910-3319
(800) 346-2742
(Series of free resource guides on basic information about a disability, including description and definition as well as treatment and resources).

Association of Birth Defect Children (ABDC)
3526 Emerywood Lane
Orlando, Florida 32812
(407) 859-2821
(Answers requests for information about birth defects from every state)

To help parents know what warning signs to look for, a brochure is available from Pathways Awareness Foundation. For a free copy, send a self-addressed stamped envelope to Pathways Awareness Foundation, 123 N. Wacker Drive, Chicago, IL 60606

CHAPTER TWO: ABOUT BIRTH DEFECTS

AUTISM

**National Autism Hotline/
Autism Services Center**
Douglass Education
Building
10th Avenue & Bruce
Huntington, W. VA 25701
(304) 525-8014

**Autism Society of
America**
1234 Massachusetts
Avenue
NW, Suite C1017
Washington, DC 20005
(202) 783-0215

BATTEN'S DISEASE

**Batten's Disease Support
and Research Association**
2600 Parsons Avenue
Columbus, OH 43207
(800) 448-4570

CEREBRAL PALSY

**United Cerebral Palsy
Association, Inc.**
7 Penn Plaza Suite 804
New York, N.Y. 10001
(800) USA-IUCP

**UCPA, Inc. National
Office**
1522 K Street, NW Suite
1112
Washington, D.C. 20005
(800) USA-5UCP

CORNELIA de LANGE
SYNDROME

**Cornelia de Lange
Syndrome Foundation**
60 Dyer Avenue
Collinsville, CT 06022
(800) 223-8355

CRI DU CHAT (CAT CRY SYNDROME)

The 5p-Society
11609 Oakmont
Overland Park, KS 66210
(913) 469-8900

CYSTIC FIBROSIS

Cystic Fibrosis Foundation
6931 Arlington Road
Bethesda, MD 20814
(800) FIGHT-CF

DOWN SYNDROME

National Down Syndrome Society
666 Broadway Suite 810
New York, N.Y. 10012
(800) 221-4602

National Down Syndrome Congress
1800 Dempster Street
Park Ridge, IL 60068-1146
(800) 232-NDSC

FRAGILE X SYNDROME

National Fragile X Foundation
1441 York Street, Suite 215
Denver CO 80206
(800) 688-8765

HEART DISORDERS

American Heart Association
7320 Greenville Avenue
Dallas, TX 75231
(214) 750-5300

HEARING IMPAIRED

Alexander Graham Bell Association for the Deaf
3417 Volta Place NW
Washington, DC 20007
(202) 337-5220
(Voice/TDD)

American Society for Deaf Children (ASDC)
814 Thayer Avenue
Silver Spring, MD 20910
(301) 585-5400

National Information Center on Deafness
Gallaudet University
800 Florida Avenue, NE
Washington, DC 20002
(202) 651-5051 (Voice) or
(202) 651-5052 (TDD)

National Association of the Deaf (NAD)
814 Thayer Avenue
Silver Spring, MD 20910
(301) 587-1788
(Voice/TDD)

HEMOPHILIA

National Hemophilia Foundation (NHF)
The Soho Building
110 Green Street, Room 406
New York, NY 10012
(212) 219-8180

HUNTINGTON'S DISEASE

Huntington's Disease Society of America, Inc.
140 West 22nd Street
New York, NY 10011-2420
(212) 242-1968
(800) 345-HDSA

Hereditary Disease Foundation
1427 Seventh Street, Suite 2
Santa Monica, CA 90401
(213) 458-4183

HYDROCEPHALUS

National Hydrocephalus Foundation
22427 S. River Road
Joliet, IL 60436
(815) 467-6548

MENTAL RETARDATION

Association for Retarded Citizens of the United States
P.O. Box 10047
Arlington, TX 76004
(817) 261-6003

MUSCULAR DYSTROPHY

Muscular Dystrophy Association
3561 E. Sunrise
Tucson, AZ 85718
(800) 223-6666

144

NATIONAL MARFAN FOUNDATION
382 Main Street
Port Washington, NY
11050
(516) 883-8712

NEUROFIBROMATOSIS

**National
Neurofibromatosis
Foundation, Inc.**
141 Fifth Avenue, Suite 7-S
New York, NY 10010
(212) 460-8980
(800) 323-7938

PREMATURE INFANTS

Parenting Preemies
P.O. Box 530
Stevens Point, WS 54481
(715) 824-2596

PRADER-WILLI SYNDROME

**Prader-Willi Syndrome
Association**
6490 Excelsior Boulevard,
E-102
St. Louis Park, MN 55426
(612) 926-1947

RARE DISEASES

**National Information
Center for Orphan Drugs
and Rare Diseases**
P.O. Box 1133
Washington, DC 20013-1133
(800) 456-3505

**National Organization for
Rare Disorders (NORD)**
P.O. Box 8923
New Fairfield, CT 06812
(203) 746-6518 or (800)
999-NORD

RETT SYNDROME

**Rett Syndrome
Association**
8511 Rose Marie Drive
Fort Washington, MD
20744
(301) 248-7031

SICKLE CELL DISEASE

**National Association for
Sickle Cell Disease, Inc.
(NASCD) 4221** Wilshire
Boulevard, #360
Los Angeles, CA 90010-
3503
(213) 936-7205 or (800)
421-8453

**National Sickle Cell
Research Foundation,
Inc.**
P.O. Box 8095
Houston, TX 77004
(713) 651-8071

SPINA BIFIDA

**Spina Bifida Association
of America**
1700 Rockville Pike, Suite
540
Rockville, ND 20852
(800) 621-3141

TAY-SACHS DISEASE

**National Tay-Sachs and
Allied Diseases
Association**
2001 Beacon Street, Suite
304
Brookline, MA 02146
(617) 277-4463

**National Foundation for
Jewish Genetic Diseases,
Inc.**
250 Park Avenue, Suite
1000
New York, NY 10017
(212) 682-5350

THALASSEMIA AND
ALLIED DISEASES

**Cooley's Anemia
Foundation**
105 East 22 Street, Suite
911
New York, N.Y. 10010
(212) 598-0911

TOURETTE SYNDROME

Tourette Syndrome Association
Park 50 TechneCenter
100 TechneCenter Drive, #116
Milford, OH 45150-2713
(513) 831-2976 or (513) 543-2675

Tourette Syndrome Association
42-40 Bell Boulevard
Bayside, NY 11361-2861
(718) 224-2999

TURNER'S SYNDROME

Turner's Syndrome Society
768-214 Twelve Oaks Center
15500 Wayzata Boulevard
Wayzata, MN 55391
(612) 475-9944

Turner's Syndrome Society
Administrative Studies Building, Room 006
4700 Keele Street-York University
Downsview, Ontario
Canada M3J 1P3
(416) 736-5023

Turner's Syndrome Society
3539 Tonkawood Road
Minnetonka, MN 55345
(612) 475-9944

VISUALLY IMPAIRED

American Council of the Blind
1010 Vermont Avenue, NW, #1100
Washington, DC 20005
(202) 393-3666 or (800) 424-8666

Retintis Pigmentosa International Society for Degenerative Eye Diseases
P.O. Box 900
Woodland Hills, CA 91365
(818) 992-0500/(800) 344-4877/(800) FIGHT-RP

WILLIAMS SYNDROME

**Williams Syndrome
Association**
P.O. Box 178373
San Diego, CA 92117-
0910
(713) 376-7072

WILSON'S DISEASE

**Wilson's Disease
Association**
P.O. Box 75324
Washington, DC 20013
(703) 636-3003

**XERODERMA
PIGMENTOSUM
REGISTRY**
UMDNJ, New Jersey
Medical School
Department of Pathology
100 Bergen Street
Newark, NJ 07103
(201) 456-6255

For additional
information contact the
**March of Dimes Birth
Defects Foundation**, 1275
Mamaroneck Avenue,
White Plains, New York
10605 (914-428-7100) or
your local chapter.

CHAPTER THREE: YOU ARE NOT ALONE

**Alliance of Genetic
Support Groups**
35 Wisconsin Circle,
Suite 440
Chevy Chase, MD 20815
(301) 652-5553 or (800)
336-GENE
AGSG provides a link to
a network of national
support groups.

**Association of Birth
Defect Children**
3526 Emerywood Lane
Orlando, FL 32812
(407) 859-2821
A national clearinghouse.

**Batten's Disease Support
Association**
2600 Parsons Avenue
Columbus, OH 43207
(800) 448-4570

**Children With Attention
Deficit Disorder (CADD)**
12493 SW 104 Lane
Miami, Florida 33186
(305) 252-0200

**Cornelia de Lange
Syndrome**
60 Dyer Avenue
Collinsville, Connecticut
06022
(800) 223-8355

Cystic Fibrosis
Cystic Fibrosis
Foundation
6931 Arlington Road
Bethesda, Maryland
20814
(800) FIGHT-CF

Down Syndrome
National Association for
Down Syndrome
P.O. Box 4542
Oak Brook, IL 60521
(312) 325-9112

**National Down Syndrome
Congress**
1800 Dempster Street
Park Ridge, IL 60068-
1146
(800) 232-NDSC

Fetal Alcohol Syndrome Resource Coalition
7802 S.E. Taylor Street
Portland, OR 97215
(503) 246-2635
Provides referrals to local support groups

Five P-Minus (CRI-du-CHAT)
The 5p-Society
11609 Oakmont
Overland Park, KS 66210
(913)469-8900

Fragile X Support, Inc.
1380 Huntington Drive
Mundelein, Illinois 60060
(312) 680-3317

Hearing Impaired
Alexander Graham Bell
Association for the Deaf
3417 Volta Place N.W.
Washington, DC 20007
(202)337-5220
International Parents
Organization

American Society for Deaf Children
814 Thayer Avenue
Silver Spring, MD 20910
(301)585-5400

Listen, Inc.
P.O. Box 27213
Tempe, AZ 85285
(602)820-8817
An association for hearing impaired children.

Human Services Research Institute
2336 Massachusetts Avenue
Cambridge, MA 02140
(617) 876-0426
Family support programs in many states.

Hydrocephalus Support Group
225 Dickinson Street, H893
San Diego, CA 92103
(619) 726-0507

Klinefelter Syndrome Associates
P.O. Box 119
Roseville, CA 95661-0119

United Leukodystrophy Foundation, Inc.
2304 Highland Drive
Sycamore, IL 60178
(815) 895-3211

National Center for Education in Maternal and Child Health (NCEMCH)
38th and R Streets, NW
Washington, DC 22057
(202) 625-8400
Provides one of the most comprehensive listings of mutual support groups concerned with birth defects.

National Information Center for Children and Youth With Handicaps
P.O. Box 1492
Washington, DC 20013
(800) 909-5599
Networks with all other organizations. Refers questions to resources in each state or community.

National Organization for Rare Disorders (NORD)
P.O. Box 8923
New Fairfield, CT 06812
(203)746-6518
(800)999-NORD

National Parent Network of Disabilities
1600 Prince Street
Suite 115
Alexandria, VA 22314
(703) 684-6763

National Neurofibromatosis Foundation, Inc.
141 Fifth Avenue, Suite 7-S
New York, NY 10010
(800) 323-7989
Support groups in United States, Australia, Canada, Finland, Hungary, Israel, Italy and Spain.

Neurofibromatosis, Inc.
3401 Woodridge Court
Mitchellville, Maryland 20716
(305) 577-8984

Parent Care, Inc.
9041 Colgate Sheet
Indianapolis, Indiana
46268
(317) 872-9913
A national organization of
parents and professionals
working to establish
parent support groups in
neonatal Intensive Care
Units.

**Parent to Parent Support
Organizations (National)**

Parents Helping Parents
535 Race Street, Suite
220
San Jose, CA 95126
(408) 288-5010

Pilot Parent Partnership
2150 E. Highland, Suite
105
Phoenix, AZ 85016
(602) 468-3001

**Parent to Parent of
Florida/Family Network
on Disabilities**
1211 Tech Blvd., Suite
105
Tampa, FL 33619
(800) 825-5736

**Parent to Parent of
Georgia, Inc.**
1644 Tullie Circle NE,
Suite 123
Atlanta, GA 30329
(404) 451-5484

Iowa Pilot Parents, Inc.
P.O. Box 1151
33 N. 12 Street
Fort Dodge, Iowa 50501
(515) 576-5870

Pilot Parents – Minnesota
201 Ordean Building
Duluth, MN 55802
(218) 726-4745

Pilot Parents
Greater Omaha ARC
3610 Dodge Street
Omaha, NE 68220
(402) 346-5220

**Family Support Network
of North Carolina**
CD7349 Trailer 31
University of North
Carolina
Chapel Hill, NC 27599-
7340
(919) 966-2841

Family First
360 S. 3rd Street, #101
Columbus, OH 43215
(614) 342-1519

Parent to Parent of Vermont
1 Main Street
69 Chaplain Mill
Winooski, VT 05405
(802) 655-5290

Parent to Parent of Virginia
Virginia Commonwealth University
301 W. Franking Street, Box 3020
Richmond, VA
(800) 344-0012

Parent to Parent Support Program
2280 8th Avenue
Seattle, WA 98121
(206) 461-7834

Rehabilitation Research and Training Center on Families and Disabilities:

The Beach Center on Families and Disability
The University of Kansas
4138 Haworth Hall
Lawrence, KS 66045
(913) 864-7600

Parent/Family Information and Support
A national source for resources in each area.
(800) 922-9234 Ext. 301

Progeria International Registry
New York State Institute for Basic Research
Department of Human Genetics
1050 Forest Hill Road
Staten Island, NY 10314
(718) 494-5230

Rubinstein-Taybi Syndrome
414 East Kansas
Smith Center, KS 66967
(913) 282-6237

SHORT STATURE

Human Growth Foundation
4720 Montgomery Lane
Bethesda, MD 20815
(301) 656-7540
(800) 451-6434

Little People of America, Inc.
P.O. Box 9897
Washington, DC 20016
(301) 589-0730

Little People of America
Parents of Dwarfed
Children
P.O. Box 633
San Bruno, CA 94066
(415) 589-0695

Parents of Dwarfed Children
11524 Colt Terrace
Silver Spring, MD 20902
(301) 649-3275

Sibling Information Network
Connecticut University
Affiliated Program
991 Main Street
Suite 3A, East
Hartford, CT 06108
(203) 282-7050

Spina Bifida Association of America
1700 Rockville Pike, Suite 540
Rockville, Maryland 20352
(800) 621-3141

Sturge-Weber Foundation
P.O. Box 460931
Aurora, CO 80015
(303) 693-2986 or (800) 621-3141

Monosomy 9p Support Group
43304 Kipton Nickle Plate Road
LaGrange, OH 44050
(216) 775-4255

Chromosome 18 Registry and Research Society
6302 Fox Head
San Antonio, TX 78247
(512) 657-4968

**Support Organization for
Trisomy 18, 13 and Other
Related Disorders
(SOFT)**
5030 Cole
Poctello, ID 83202
(203)237-8782
 or
Barb Van Herreweghe
2982 S. Union Street
Rochester, NY 14624
(716) 594-4621

TAY-SACHS DISEASE

**National Tay-Sachs and
Allied Diseases
Association**
2001 Beacon's, Suite 304
Brookline, MA 02140
(617) 277-4463
Parent peer group of
mutual support.

**Turner's Syndrome
Society**
768-214 Twelve Oaks
Center
15500 Wayzata Boulevard
Wayzata, MN 55391
(612) 475-9944

**Turner's Syndrome
Society**
Administrative Studies
Building, Room 006
4700 Keele Street-York
University
Downsview, Ontario
Canada M3J 1P3
(416) 736-5023

**Turner's Syndrome
Society**
3539 Tonkawood Road
Minnetonka, MN 55345
(612) 475-9944

**United Cerebral Palsy
Association**
7 Penn Plaza, Suite 804
New York, N.Y. 10001
(800) USA-1UCP

**The USA Sotos Syndrome
Parent Support Group**
c/o Marilyn Brandon
Research and Education
Scott and White Clinic
2401 South 31st Street
Temple, TX 76508
(817) 774-2350

**Soto Syndrome Support
Association**
Jean Nesket-Dowe, Pres.
797 W. Lockwood Blvd.
Glendale, Missouri 63122
(314) 966-4194

VISUAL IMPAIRMENT

**National Association for
Parents of the Visually
Impaired 2180** Linway
Drive
Beloit, WI 53511
(800) 562-6265 or (608)
362-4945

**Williams Syndrome
Association**
1611 Claton Spur Court
Ellisville, MO 63011
(314) 227-4411

**Xeroderma Pigmentosum
Support Group**
P.O. Box 431
Yuba City, CA 95991
(916) 696-0328

CHAPTER FOUR: THEN AND NOW

Parents can check with special education directors or the principal in their local school system to find out what is available for their child. For a listing of information sources in your state about the Federally funded Parent Information and Training Program, contact the National Information Center for Children and Youth with Handicaps, NICHCY (800)999-5999.

You may also look for help in your community through United Cerebral Palsy Association. If you are near a center for infant development, you can enroll your child, even under age three.

In addition, other centers operate under different auspices. If you need help in locating one, contact the Association for Retarded Citizens, Easter Seals or the Bureau of Education for the Handicapped. (U. S. Office of Education, 400 Maryland Avenue, SE, Washington, DC 20202.)

For referrals to appropriate specialists and therapists contact the National Health Information Clearinghouse, P.O. Box 1133, Washington, DC 20013 (800-336-4797).

157

Anne Carlsen School
301 7th Avenue, NW
Jamestown, ND 58401
(701) 252-3850 (Ages 3-21)

The Devereux Foundation
19 South Waterloo Road
Box 400
Devon, PA 19333
(800) 345-1292 x3045 or
(215) 964-3045
(Childhood-Geriatric)

Kluge Children's Rehabilitation Center
2270 Ivy Road
Charlottesville, VA 22901
(804) 924-5161 (Birth to 21)

Institutes for the Achievement of Human Potential
8801 Stenton Avenue
Philadelphia, PA 19118
(215) 233-2050

St. Coletta School
W4955 Highway 18
Jefferson, WI 53549
(414) 674-4330 (Ages 6 & Up)

Office of Special Education and Rehabilitation Services
Clearinghouse on Disability Information
U.S. Department of Education
Switzer Building, 330 C Street, SW
Washington, DC 20202
(202) 732-1723 or (202) 732-1245

(American Council on Rural) Special Education (ACRES)
Western Washington University
Bellingham, WA 98225
(206) 676-3576

**National Network of
Parent Centers**
TAPP Project
312 Stuart Street, 2nd
Floor
Boston, MA 02116
(617) 482-2915
Provides technical
assistance for parent
programs to meet the
educational needs of
children with special
needs. Delivery of
technical assistance is
arranged through the four
TAPP Regional Centers:

**Washington State PAVE
(West Region)**
Parents Advocating for
Vocational Education
6316 South 12th Street
Tacoma, WA 98465
(206) 565-2266

**PACER Center (Midwest
Region)**
Parent Advocacy
Coalition for Educational
Rights
4826 Chicago Avenue,
South
Minneapolis, MN 55417
(612) 827-2966

(Northeast Region)
Parent Information
Center
P.O. Box 1422
Concord, NH 03302
(603) 224-6299

**Parents Educating
Parents (PEP) Project
(South Region)**
Georgia Association for
Retarded Citizens
1851 Ram Runway, Suite
104
College Park, GA 30337
(404) 761-3150

**Parent Training and
Information Centers**
Nearly every state has an
organization funded by
the Federal Government.

**Special Education Action
Committee, Inc.**
P.O. Box 161274
Mobile, AL 36606
(205) 478-1208

Pilot Parents, Inc.
2150 East Highland
Avenue
Phoenix, AZ 85016
(602) 468-3001

Arkansas Coalition for the Handicapped
519 East Capitol
Little Rock, AR 72202
(501) 376-3420

Focus
2917 King Street, Suite C
Jonesboro, AR 72401
(501) 935-2750

Task
18685 Santa Inez
Fountain Valley, CA 92708
(714) 962-6332

Parents Helping Parents
535 Race Street, Suite 220
San Jose, CA 95126
(408) 288-5010

DREDF
2212 6th Street
Berkeley, CA 94710
(415) 644-2555

Disability Services Matrix
P.O. Box 6541
San Rafael, CA 94903
(415) 499-3877

Peak
6055 Lehman Drive, #101
Colorado Springs, CO 80918
(719) 531-9400

CT Parent Advocacy Center
P.O. Box 579
East Lyme, CT 06333
(203) 739-3089

PIC of Delaware, Inc.
700 Barksdale Road, Suite 6
Newark, DE 19711
(302) 366-0152

Parent Education Network/Florida, Inc.
1211 Tech Blvd., Suite 105
Tampa, FL 33619
(813) 238-6100 or (800) 825-5736

Parents Education Parents (PEP)
Georgia ARC
1851 Ram Runway, #104
College Park, GA 30337
(404) 761-2745

Idaho Parents United, Inc.
6816 Fernwood Drive
Boise, ID 83709
(208) 377-2199

Coordinating Council for Handicapped Children
20 East Jackson
Boulevard, Room 900
Chicago, IL 60604
(312) 922-0317

Task Force on Education for the Handicapped, Inc.
833 Northside Boulevard
Building 1, Rear
South Bend, IN 46617
(219) 234-7101

Iowa Exceptional Parents Center
33 North 12th Street
P.O. Box 1151
Fort Dodge, IA 50501

Families Together, Inc.
4125 S. W. Gage Center
Drive, Suite 200
Topeka, KS 66604
(913) 273-6343

Kentucky Special Parent Involvement Network
318 West Kentucky Street
Louisville, KY 40203
(502) 587-5717 or (502) 584-1104

United Cerebral Palsy of Greater New Orleans
1500 Edwards Avenue, Suite O
Harahan, LA 70123
(504) 733-7736

Special Needs Parent Information Network (SPIN)
P.O. Box 2067
Augusta, ME 04330
(207) 582-2504 or (800) 325-0220

Federation for Children with Special Needs
312 Stuart Street, 2nd Floor
Boston, MA 02116
(617) 482-2915

Rainbow of Hope: A Guide for the Special Needs Child

United Cerebral Palsy
Detroit Community
Service Department
17000 West 8 Mile Road,
Suite 380
Southfield, MI 48075
(313) 557-5070

**Citizens Alliance to
Uphold Special Education
(CAUSE)**
313 South Washington,
Square Lower Level
Lansing, MI 48933
(517) 485-4084 or (800)
221-9105 (MI only)

PACER Center, Inc.
4826 Chicago Avenue,
South
Minneapolis, MN 55417
(612) 827-2966 or (800)
53-PACER (MN only)

**Association of
Developmental
Organizations of
Mississippi**
332 New Market Drive
Jackson, MS 39209
(601) 922-3210 or (800)
231-3721

**Missouri Parents Act
(MPACT)**
1722 W. South Glenstone,
Suite 125
Springfield, MO 65804
(417) 882-7434 or (800)
66-MPACT

**Missouri Parents Act
(MPACT)**
625 Euclid, #225
St. Louis, MO 63108
(314) 361-1660

**Parents, Let's Unite for
Kids (EMC/MCHC)**
1500 North 30th Street
Billings, MT 59101-0298
(406) 657-2055

**Nebraska Parent
Information Training
Center**
3610 Dodge Street
Omaha, NE 68131
(402) 346-5220

**Parent Information
Center**
151A Manchester Street
P.O. Box 1422
Concord, NH 03302
(603) 224-6299

**Statewide Parent
Advocacy Network, Inc.
(SPAN)**
516 North Avenue, East
Westfield, NJ 07090
(201) 654-7726

EPICS Project
P.O. Box 788
Bernalillo, NM 87004
(505) 867-3396

**Parents Reaching Out to
Help**
1127 University, NE
Albuquerque, NM 87102
(505) 842-9405

**Parent Networking Center
(PNC)**
1443 Main Street
Buffalo, NY 14209
(716) 885-1004

Advocates for Children
New York City
Organization/Special
Education
24-16 Bridge Plaza, South
Long Island City, NY
11101
(718) 729-8866

**Exceptional Children's
Advocacy Council**
P.O. Box 16
Davidson, NC 28036
(704) 892-1321

**Pathfinder Services of
North Dakota**
16th Street & 2nd
Avenue
SW Arrowhead Shopping
Center
Minot, ND 58701
(701) 268-3390

SOC Information Center
106 Wellington Place,
#LL
Cincinnati, OH 45219
(513) 381-2400

**Ohio Coalition for the
Education of
Handicapped Children**
933 high Street, Suite 106
Worthington, OH 43085
(614) 431-1307

163

Parents Reaching Out in Oklahoma Project
1917 South Harvard Avenue
Oklahoma City, OK 73128
(405) 681-9710 or (800) PL9-4142

Oregon COPE Project
999 Locust Street, NE#42
Salem, OR 97303
(503) 373-7477
(Voice/TDD)

Parents Union for Public Schools
401 North Broad Street, #916
Philadelphia, PA 19108
(215) 574-0337

Parent Advisory Council
c/o Riverview Inter/Unit PD #2
Shippenville, PA 16254
(814) 677-3751

Association of Retarded Citizens of Tennessee
1805 Hayes Street, Suite 100
Nashville, TN 37203
(615) 327-0294

PATH
7475 Calder Avenue, #202
Beaumont, TX 77707
(409) 866-4726

Utah PIC
2290 East 4500 South, #110
Salt Lake City, UT 84117
(801) 272-1051 or (800) 468-1160

VT Information and Training Network
Vermont/ARC
37 Champlain Mill
Winooski, VT 05404
(802) 655-4016

Parent Education Advocacy Training Center
228 South Pitt Street, #300
Alexandria, VA 22314
(703) 836-2953

Washington PAVE
6316 S. 12th Street
Tacoma, WA 98465
(206) 565-2266
(Voice/TDD) or (800) 5-PARENT

Specialized Training of Military Parents (PAVE/STOMP)
12208 Pacific Highway, SW
Tacoma, WA 98499
(206) 588-1741

Parent Education Project
United Cerebral Palsy of SE Wisconsin
230 West Wells Street, #502
Milwaukee, WI 53202
(414) 272-4500

Carmen Selles Vila
Asociacion De Padres Pro Biene Star/Ninos Impedidos de PR, Inc.
P.O. Box 21301
Rio Piedras, PR 00928
(809) 763-4665/765-0345

Americans With Disabilities Act
For more information, call or write your U.S. Senator or Representative for a copy of P.L.101 336(ADA)

President's Committee on Employment of the Handicapped
1111 20th Street, NW – Suite 636
Washington, DC 20036-3470
(202) 653-5044/653-5050 (TDD)

The Supplemental Security Income (SSI) program has made it easier for needy disabled children under 18 to qualify. To apply, a family should contact the nearest Social Security district office. A booklet, "SSI: New Opportunities for Children with Disabilities" is available from:

Mental Health Law Project
1101 Fifteenth Street, NW
Suite 1212
Washington, D.C. 20005

National Lekotek Center
2100 Ridge Avenue
Evanston, Illinois 60201
(708) 328-0001

CHAPTER FIVE: SPECIAL CHILDREN
SPECIAL FAMILIES

There are magazines geared to parenting a child with a disability:

Exceptional Parent
P.O. Box 3000
Department EP
Denville, New Jersey
07834-9919

New Ways
P.O. Box 5072
Evanston, Illinois 60204

Check with your local library for books about specific disabilities or other materials related to special needs children.

Special Parent/Special Child
Lindell Press, Inc.
P.O. Box 462
South Salem, NY 10590
Bi-monthly newsletter focuses on topics relevant to the needs of special parents.

On Becoming a Special Parent:
Parent/Professional Publications
P.O. Box 59730
Chicago, Illinois 60645

Parent Consultants
411 Locust Road
Wilmette, Illinois 60091
(708) 251-3613

CHAPTER SIX: AT HOME AND AWAY FROM HOME

For information on group home or residential facility, contact state office of the Developmental Disabilities Council or local chapter of ARC.

Directory on Public Facilities:
Central Wisconsin Center for the Developmentally Disabled
317 Knutson Drive
Madison, WI 53704
(608) 249-2151

Directory on Private Facilities:
National Association of Private Residential Facilities for the Mentally Retarded
4200 Evergreen Lane, Suite 315
Annandale, VA 22003
(703) 642-6614

Directory of both Private and Public Facilities:
Directory for Exceptional Children
Porter Sargent Publishers
11 Beacon Street
Boston, MA 02108
(617) 523-1670

National Association of Private Schools for Exceptional Children (NAPSEC)
1625 I Street, Suite 506
Washington, DC 20006
(202) 223-2192

Berkshire Children's Community
41 Taconic Avenue
Great Barrington, MA 01230
(413) 528-2523

Elwyn
111 Elwyn Road
Elwyn, PA 19063
(800) 345-8111

**HMS School for Children
with Cerebral Palsy**
4400 Baltimore Avenue
Philadelphia, PA 19104
(215) 222-2566

Hope Center
666 S. W. Fourth Street
Miami, FL 33130
(305) 545-7572

The Hope School
50 Hazel Lane
Springfield, IL 62716
(217) 786-3350

Institute of Logopedics
2400 Jardine Drive
Wichita, KS 67219
(800) 835-1043
(Ages 6-11)

Keystone
406 N. Washington
Avenue
Scranton, PA 18503
(717) 346-7561

Little City Foundation
1760 West Algonquin
Road
Palatine, IL 60067-4799
(708) 358-5510

New England Villages
664 School Street
Pembroke, MA 02359
(617) 293-5461

Ohel Children's Home
4423 16th Avenue
Brooklyn, NY 11204
(718) 851-6300

Pathfinder Village
R.R. 1, Box 32A
Edmeston, NY 13335
(607) 965-8377

Stewart Home School
Box 20
Frankfort, KY 40601
(502) 875-4664

Sunrise
22300 S. W. 162nd
Avenue
Miami, FL 33170
(305) 245-6150

**National Council on
Independent Living**
2539 Telegraph Avenue
Berkeley, CA 94704
(415) 849-1243

**National Rehabilitation
Information Center**
8455 Colesville Road,
Suite 935
Silver Springs, MD 20910-
3319
(Puts out newsletter of
disability and
rehabilitation research
resources.)

**National Council on the
Handicapped**
800 Independence
Avenue, SW, Suite 184
Washington, DC 20591

**National Parent Resource
Center**
Federation for Children
with Special Needs
95 Berkeley Street, Suite
104
Boston, MA 02116
(617) 482-2915
(Provides national
coordination with regional
groups.)

**National Catholic Office
for Persons with
Disabilities**
P.O. Box 29113
Washington, DC 20017
(202) 259-2933

**National Organization on
Disability**
910 16th Street NW,
Suite 600
Washington, DC 20006
(202) 293-5960

**National Parent Network
on Disabilities**
1600 Prince St., Suite 115
Alexandria, VA 22314
(703) 684-6763

National Park Service
Division of Special
Programs
P.O. Box 37127
Washington, DC 20013
(202) 343-4747

SERVICES:

IBM National Support Center for Persons with Disabilities
P.O. Box 2150
Atlanta, GA 30055
(800) 426-2133
(A clearinghouse and advocacy center that keeps information on almost 800 computer-related devices for hundreds of companies and can refer callers to more than 900 other organizations that serve the handicapped.)

Apple Computer's Office of Special Education and Rehabilitation
(408) 974-7910
(Maintaining an extensive database of information describing hardware, software, organizations and publications for disabled people. Any Apple dealer can gain access to it for more information.)

AT&T National Special Needs Center
(800) 233-1222
(Provides information about special telephones, TDD machines for the deaf and other personal computer communications devices.)

RESPITE SERVICES:

National Information Center for Children and Youth with Disabilities
P.O. Box 1492
Washington, D.C. 20013
(800) 999-5599
(NICHCY provides free information and will send a copy of their news digest, ND12 Respite Care: A Gift of Time, and a resource list for your state.

DIRECTORY OF CAMP GUIDES:

American Camping Association
5000 State Road 67 North
Martinsville, IN 46151
(317) 342-8456

**Camps for Kids Muncy
Manuscripts**
P.O. Box 1561
Grapeville, TX 76051
(817) 329-0060

**Camping for the
Handicapped**
2056 South Buffalo Road
Traverse City, MI 49684

**DIRECTORY OF
SUMMER CAMPS:**

**The Parent Information
Center**
P.O. Box 1422
Concord, NH 03302
(603) 224-7005
(This is a comprehensive
listing of summer camps
that accept disabled
students and children
{$11.50}.)

**Directory of Summer
Camps for Children with
Learning Disabilities
(ACALD)**
4156 Library Road
Pittsburgh, PA 15234
(412) 341-1515/9077
(The cost for the
directory is $3.00)

**Annual Special Camp
Guide Resources for
Children with Special
Needs**
200 Park Avenue South,
Suite 816
New York, NY 10003
(212) 677-4650

**Guide to Summer Camps
and Summer Schools**
Porter Sargeant
11 Beacon Street
Boston, MA 02108
(617) 523-1670

AHRC Camping Services
200 Park Avenue South
New York, NY 10003
(212) 254-82031, Ext. 250

**Access America: An Atlas
and Guide to the
National Parks for
Visitors with Disabilities**
Northern Cartographic,
Inc.
Dept. AA-91 P.O. Box
133
Burlington, VT 05401
(802) 860-2886

National Park Camping Guide
Superintendent of Documents
US Government Printing Office
Washington, DC 20402
(202) 783-3238
($3.50 when ordering, use stock number 024-005-00987-6)

Parents Guide to Accredited Camps
American Camping Association
Bradford Woods
500 State Road 67 North
Martinsville, IN 46151
(317) 342-8456
($9.50 This directory includes a list of specialized camps for children with disabilities.)

Residential Camping Programs List
National Easter Seal Society
2023 West Ogden Avenue
Chicago, IL 60612
(312) 243-8400 or (312) 243-8880 (TDD) (Free)

Guide to Summer Residential Programs for Individuals with Disabilities
Information Center for Individuals with Disabilities (ICID) 20 Park Plaza, Room 330
Boston, MA 02116
(617) 727-5540
(The cost is $10.00)
Check at Public Library for American Camp Association list of handicapped organizations.

Special Olympics
1350 New York Avenue, NW, Suite 500
Washington, DC 20005-4709
(202) 628-3630

North American Riding for the Handicapped Association 1-800-369-RIDE.
Request the phone number for a program in your area.

Boy Scouts of America
Scouting for the
Handicapped
1325 Walnut Hill Lane
P.O. Box 152079
Irving, TX 75015
(214) 580-2000

Girl Scouts
830 3rd Avenue & 51st
Street
New York, NY 10022
(212) 940-7500

For books on accessible
travel contact:
The Disability Bookshop
P.O. Box 129
Vancouver, WA 98666
(206) 694-2462

Toys for Special Children
385 Warburton Avenue
Hastings, NY 10706
(914) 478-0960

CHAPTER SEVEN: ADOPTION, THE ANSWER FOR SOME

National Adoption Center
1218 Chestnut Street
Philadelphia, PA 19107
(800) TO-ADOPT
(Promotes adoption of
special needs children.)

**National Adoption
Information
Clearinghouse**
CSR, Inc.
1400 Eye (I) Street, NW,
Suite 600
Washington, DC 20005
(202) 842-7600

**National Committee for
Adoption**
1930 17th Street, NW
Washington, DC 20009
(202) 328-1200

**North American Council
on Adoptable Children**
1821 University Ave. W.
#N498
St. Paul, MN 55104
(Adoptive parent support
group.)

**National Resources
Center on Special Needs
Adoption**
P.O. Box 337
Chelsea, MI 48118
(313) 475-8693

**AASK America – Aid to
Adoption of Special Kids**
657 Mission Street, Suite
601
San Francisco, California
94105
(800) 447-5400

**Catholic Social Services
of Wisconsin**
1825 Riverside Drive
P.O. Box 1825
Green Bay, Wisconsin
54805-5825

**Child Welfare League of
America, Inc.**
440 First Street N.W.,
Suite 310
Washington, D.C. 20001
(202) 638-2952

Resource List

**Jewish Children's
Adoption Network**
P.O. Box 16544
Denver, Colorado 80210-
8544
(303) 573-8113

**Jewish Child Care
Association**
575 Lexington Avenue
New York, N.Y. 10022
(212) 371-1313

**New York Spaulding for
Children**
121 West 27th Street
New York, N.Y. 10011
(212) 645-7610

**Spina Bifida Association
of America**
1700 Rockville Pike, Suite
540
Rockville, Maryland
20852
(800) 621-3141

**Adoptive Families of
America**
3333 Highway 100N
Minneapolis, MN 55422
(612) 535-4829
(National Umbrella
Organization)

**Down Syndrome Adoptive
Exchange**
56 Midchester Avenue
White Plains, NY 10606
(914) 428-1236

**Up with Down Syndrome
Foundation**
9270 Hammocks
Boulevard, Suite 301
Miami, FL 33196
(305) 252-2552

Check local Religious,
Social and Family
Services and Department
of Health and
Rehabilitative Services.

175

CHAPTER EIGHT: BRAVE NEW WORLD

**Office of Orphan
Products Development**
Food and Drug
Administration
5600 Fishers Lane
Rockville, MD 20857

**National Institutes of
Health**
Bethesda, MD 20892

Research! America
(800) 366-2873

**Immune Deficiency
Foundation**
P.O. Box 586
Columbia, MD 21045

CHAPTER NINE: GENETIC COUNSELING

Alliance of Genetic Support Groups
1001-22 Street N.W., Suite 800
Washington, DC 20037
(800) 336-GENE

National Society of Genetic Counselors
233 Canterbury Drive
Wallingford, Pennsylvania 19086
(215) 872-7608

National Center for Education in Maternal and Child Health
38th and R Streets N.W.
Washington, DC 22057
(202) 625-8400

March of Dimes Birth Defects Foundation
1275 Mamaroneck Avenue
White Plains, New York 10605
(914) 428-7100
Referrals and free publications on genetic diseases and birth defects.

For information and genetic counseling for deaf individuals and families:
Gallaudet Research Institute
800 Florida Avenue, NE
Washington, DC 20002
(800) 451-8834

National Foundation for Jewish Genetic Disease
250 Park Avenue, #1000
New York, NY 10017
(212) 682-5550

CHAPTER TEN: THE FUTURE IS NOW

**National Network to
Prevent Birth Defects**
P.O. Box 15309,
Southeast Station
Washington, DC 20003

**Pregnancy/Environmental
Hotline**
National Birth Defects
Center
30 Warren Street
Boston, MA 02135
(800) 322-5014

**Office of Disease
Prevention**
National Health
Information Center
P.O. Box 1133
Washington, DC 20013-
1133
(800) 336-4797

**Association of Birth
Defect Children**
3526 Emerywood Lane
Orlando, FL 32812
(407) 859-2821

INDEX

ABOUT THE AUTHOR

Toby Levin is a freelance journalist who has been a feature writer, contributing editor and columnist for magazines and newspapers. She was an account executive for a public relations firm and is a member of the Florida Freelance Writers Association. In 1991, she presented an abstract on Genetic Support Groups at the 8th International Congress on Human Genetics.

ACKNOWLEDGMENTS

Many special people helped make this book a reality. I have interviewed geneticists, medical experts, researchers, psychologists, and last but not least, parents and their special needs children.

Special thanks go to the researchers who are the real heroes in the battle to cure birth defects. They work backstage, far away from the spotlight, but are shining lights in their dedication to helping others.

I thank the people and organizations already mentioned and so many others for their input. But, it is the parents who have been an invaluable resource by sharing their experiences and the children who were my inspiration.

In this last decade of the 20th century, the Human Genome Project is unlocking the door to the mysterious world of birth defects. Recent discoveries are opening that door wider and will continue to bring more hope than ever before.

Although the author and publisher have researched all sources to ensure the accuracy and completeness of the information contained in this book, we assume no responsibility for errors, inaccuracies, omissions or any inconsistency herein. Any slights of people or organizations are unintentional.

This book is available at special quantity discount for organizations or fund-raising. For quotes on quantity purchases, please write or call Starlight Publishing Company, Inc., 1893 N.E. 164 Street, Suite 100, North Miami Beach, Florida 33162. (305) 944-8446

BOOK REVIEWS

"This guide will empower parents who are devastated by a diagnosis of disability to regain control over their children's destinies because it provides information on causes and therapies for common and rare disabilities. It's emphasis on services and support and its extensive resources guide make it a significant contribution to the self-help literature on parenting. RECOMMENDED."

The Library Journal, February, 1992

* * * * *

"This brand new book features lots of information and encouragement to parents. Includes listings of local and national groups."

The Parent Press, a newsletter for parents of special needs children.

* * * * *

"RAINBOW OF HOPE: A Guide for the Special Needs Child was written as a means of helping families deal with the challenges placed on them when their child is born with a birth defect."

From the *5P- Society* newsletter